·

An Introduction
to the
Study of the Tarot

by Paul Foster Case

As an erudite book, all combinations of which reveal the harmonies preexisting between signs and numbers, the practical value of the Tarot is truly and above all marvelous - Eliphas Levi

ISBN-10: 1936690837
ISBN-13: 978-1-936690-83-1

Originally published in New York, 1920

THE TREE OF LIFE

and the

TWENTY-TWO PATHS OF THE SEPHER YETZIRAH

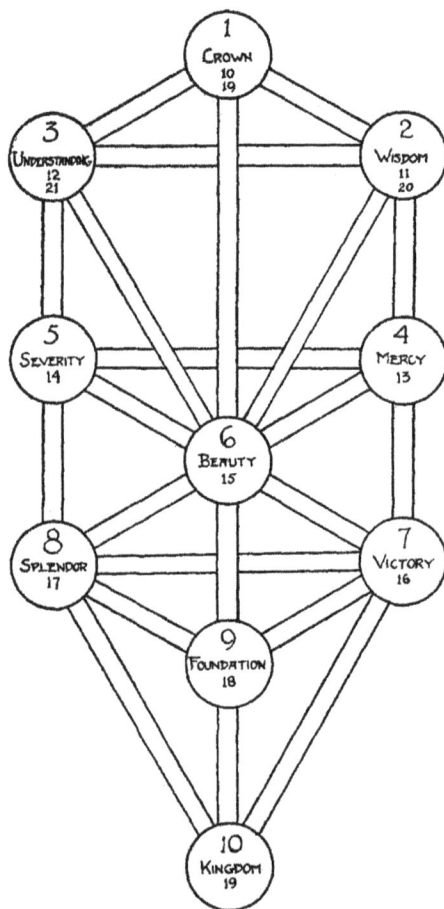

Preface

This book aims to show how to use the Tarot cards for the purpose of evoking thought, and thus bringing to the surface of the student's consciousness those great, fundamental principles of Occult Science which lie hidden in the hearts of all mankind. All these principles are based upon a single truth, and knowledge of that truth is innate in every human being; but not until it has been found and brought into the light of consciousness is it available for use. Hence the portals of ancient temples bore the motto, "Know Thyself;" hence Jesus said, "Seek first the kingdom of God, which is within you;" and Eckhartshausen declared: "As infinity in numbers loses itself in the unit which is their basis, and as the innumerable rays of a circle, are united in a single center, so it is also with the Mysteries; their hieroglyphics and infinitude of emblems have the object of exemplifying but one single truth. He who knows this has found the key to understand everything, and all at once."

Its rich symbolism and ingenious construction make the Tarot the best of all instruments for true occult education, i. e., for "drawing out" the wisdom hidden in the heart of man. Proper interpretation of these symbols, however, requires sonic knowledge of the elements of the Qabalah. The student will find these essentials in the first four chapters of this book. In connection with them, the frontispiece should be studied very carefully, for it is, in very truth, a key to all things occult.

The circles are the ten Sephiroth. Their numbers are printed above their names, and these are also the numbers of the Tarot trumps from the Magician to the Wheel of Fortune. Below the Sephirotic titles are the numbers of the major trumps which also correspond to those Sephiroth.

To those critics who may complain that my interpretations of the Tarot differ widely from most of those published hitherto, I would point out the fact that nearly all the explanations of the Tarot that have found their way into print have been based upon the false attribution of the cards to the Hebrew alphabet, used by Eliphas Levi. He undoubtedly knew the true attribution, but for reasons which probably seemed to him sufficient, deliberately concealed it.

This is not the place to discuss those reasons; but for the benefit of any who may question my wisdom in publishing this attribution, let me say that I received it from no one. Following Court de Gebelin, who makes the zero card head the series of major trumps, and Levi, who says the cards illustrate the occult meaning of the Hebrew alphabet, I worked out this system some twelve years ago; and I believe that its results in the interpretation of the symbolism are sufficient evidence of its accuracy.

Finally, I have said nothing of the divinatory uses of the Tarot, not because I agree with those who deprecate its application to the art of divination; but rather because it is my belief that the best results in foretelling the future with the Tarot can he obtained by none who are not thoroughly grounded in the philosophy of the cares. Familiarity with their astrological meanings is practically indispensable for accurate divination. I hope, at some future time, to publish a work devoted exclusively to the astrological and divinatory uses of this remarkable alphabet of symbols.

New York City, December, 1919.   PAUL FOSTER CASE.

Table of Contents

Preface..3
Contents..5
CHAPTER I...6
CHAPTER II...10
CHAPTER III...15
CHAPTER IV...22
CHAPTER V...28
CHAPTER VII..38
CHAPTER VIII..43
CHAPTER IX...49
CHAPTER X...54
CHAPTER XI...59
CHAPTER XII..65

CHAPTER I

For five centuries or more Tarot cards have been used in Europe, ostensibly for games and fortune-telling, but really to preserve the essentials of a secret doctrine. They form a symbolic alphabet of the ancient wisdom, and to their influence upon the minds of a few enlightened thinkers we may trace the modern revival of interest in that wisdom.

This revival may be said to date from 1854, when Eliphas Levi published Dogme et Rituel de la Haute Magie, the first of a series of occult books in which he named the Tarot as his most important source of information. His influence appears in the writings of H. P. Blavatsky; it pervades the teachings of the French occult school, headed by Papus (Dr. Gerard Encausse); it is developed for English readers in the works of S. L. MacGregor Mathers, A. E. Waite, Dr. W. Wynn Westcott, and others; it enters the New Thought movement in various ways, notably through the essays of Judge Troward, and it even extends to Scottish Rite Masonry in the United States, by way of Albert Pike's Morals and Dogma, which repeats verbatim passage after passage from Levi's Dogme et Rituel.

Levi's opinion of the Tarot was very high. He recommended it to occult students as a key to all mysteries. "A prisoner devoid of books," he declared, "had he only a Tarot of which he knew how to make use, could in a few years acquire a universal science, and converse with an unequalled doctrine and inexhaustible eloquence.[1]

My aim is to show my readers how to use the Tarot. An exhaustive treatment of this subject would fill many volumes; but I hope to fulfill the promise of my title by giving a concise explanation of the general plan of the Tarot, and a brief interpretation of its emblems. Let it be understood, however, that this is merely an outline. which the student must complete with the results of his own observation and meditation.

A Tarot pack contains seventy-eight cards. Fifty-six - minor trumps, or lesser arcana - are divided into four suits: wands (clubs), cups (hearts), swords (spades) and pentacles (diamonds). Each suit includes four court cards - king, queen, knight and page - and ten spot cards, numbered from ace

---

1 Mysteries of Magic, London, 1897, p. 285

to ten. The spots, usually grouped in geometrical designs, are sometimes combined with pictures illustrating the divinatory meanings of the cards. The rest of the pack - major trumps, or greater arcana - is a series of symbolic pictures. Each has a special title, and bears a number.

The doctrine behind these symbols has assumed many forms. The Vedas are its oldest literary expression, but it was known, and transmitted orally from generation to generation, long before the Vedas passed into writing. In one sense it is that true Christian religion which, according to St. Augustine, always existed, and only began to be called Christian after the time of Jesus. It is the truth taught by such organized schools as the Rosicrucians and Craft Masonry, and by the Great School from which these and other similar societies have proceeded. It is veiled also by the symbols of alchemy and astrology. Hence the Tarot speaks many languages, and its emblems are full of meaning to every student of the ancient mysteries, no matter by what path he may have approached the truth which is at the heart of them all. Yet, though its symbolism is catholic, because it expresses universal ideas, the Tarot also represents a particular version of the sacred science., It is a symbolic alphabet of the occult philosophy of Israel-an emblematic synthesis of the Qabalah.

Its major trumps illustrate the occult meaning of the twenty- two Hebrew letters, as given in the Sepher Yetzirah. Much depends, therefore, on making sure that each is assigned to the letter. The numbers of the cards enable us to do this. Twenty-one are numbered consecutively, beginning with one. Obviously, they must follow each other in the order of their numbers. The whole problem, therefore, hinges upon the disposition of the other card, which sometimes has no number, but usually bears the zero-sign.

Eliphas Levi, probably to mystify uninitiated readers, puts it between the trumps numbered twenty and twenty-one. Others make it follow the twenty-first card. But if we ask, "What comes after twenty-one?" the answer is "Twenty-two," while if our question be, "What precedes one?" the reply is, "Nothing." Logically, then the zero card should be first in the series of major trumps, preceding the card bearing the number 1. It corresponds, therefore, to the first Hebrew letter, Aleph, and the rest of the major trumps are assigned to the remaining Hebrew letters in the natural order of their numbers.

Turning our attention to the minor trumps, let us begin with the symbolism of the four suits. They represent the four worlds, or planes of existence, which, in the Qabalah, are said to constitute the universe. Each world has its own characteristic activity, and is the abode of a principle of the human constitution. is typified by one of the "living creatures" mentioned in Ezekiel and Revelation; and as each creature represents one of the four cardinal signs of the zodiac, the suits are also symbols for those signs and for the occult elements" to which they correspond. The complete meaning of the suits is as follows:

> WANDS: Atziluth, archetypal world; spirit; lion; Leo; fire. CUPS: Briah, creative world; soul; eagle, Scorpio; water.
> SWORDS. Yetzirah, formative world; astral body; man; Aquarius; air. PENTACLES: Assiah,, material world; material body; bull; Taurus; earth.

In each world are manifested ten "numerations," or Sephiroth, emanations from the Inscrutable Source of all existence (אין סוף אור), Ain Suph "No Limit." Each Sephirah has a name, and is the seat of a particular manifestation of intelligence.

They are:

1. Kether (כתר)   Crown; Hidden Intelligence.

2. Chokmah (חכמה) Wisdom; Illuminating Intelligence.

3. Binah (בינה)   Understanding; Sanctifying Intelligence.

4. Chesed (חסד)   Mercy; Measuring Intelligence.

5. Geburah (גבורה)   Strength; Radical Intelligence.

6. Tiphareth (תפארת) Beauty; Intelligence of the Mediating Influence.

7. Netzach (נצח)   Victory; Occult Intelligence.

8. Hod (הוד)   Splendor; Perfect Intelligence.

9. Yesod (יסוד)   Foundation; Pure Intelligence.

10. Malkuth (מלכות) Kingdom, or Realization; Resplendent Intelligence.

These emanations are symbolized by the numbered cards of the minor trumps. Each suit of spot cards represents the Sephiroth or one of the four worlds. The court cards denote the four principles of the human constitution. Kings typify the spirit; queens represent the soul; knights correspond to the astral body; and pages symbolize the physical body. There are four of each, because each principle manifests simultaneously in all four worlds. Such is the general outline of the correspondence of the Tarot to the main points of the Qabalah. The student in whom this introductory chapter has aroused a desire to learn the deeper meanings of the Tarot should get the pack designed by Miss Pamela Coleman Smith, under the supervision of Mr. A. E. Waite.

It is by far the best, and I shall make it the basis of the interpretations to be given in later chapters. It may be had from the publishers of AZOTH. Having procured the cards, let the student consider the various attributions, with the corresponding Tarots before him. Thus he will discover many things I have no space to mention in these pages. Let him, in particular, write out the full meaning of each minor trump, as indicated by its number and suit. It is really surprising how soon the fundamental propositions of the Qabalah may be memorized by this method. After finishing this preparatory work, the student will be ready to use the great key to the Tarot-a key mentioned by Eliphas Levi, which Papus attempted to use in preparing his Tarot of the Bohemians, but failed, because he employed an incorrect attribution of the major trumps to the Hebrew alphabet. This key is the sacred name, commonly rendered Jehovah in English. An interpretation of its meaning, and an explanation of its application to the Tarot will be found in the next chapter.

CHAPTER II

The great name of the God of Israel occurs more than five thousand times in the Bible.

Qabalists call it the Tetragrammaton, or quadrilateral name. Other divine names, such as ADNI, AHIH, and AGLA, also contain four letters, but there is only one Tetragrammaton. It is spelt Yod-Heh-Vau-Heh- in English letters, I-H-V-H.

The Bible ascribes peculiar power to this name; and tradition says that to pronounce it is to possess. a key to all wisdom.[2] In the occult sense, to pronounce the name is to -rasp its inner meaning. It is really a cipher, which conceals the profoundest mysteries of Qabalistic doctrine.

The Tarot of the Bohemians gives a brief interpretation of this name and shows how the four letters correspond to the occult meaning of numbers. To it I am indebted for my first knowledge of these matters; but in considering how Yod-Heh- Vau-Heh unlocks the mysteries of the Tarot, I hope to bring to light facts that have not been published before.

My object is neither to prove the accuracy of the Qabalistic interpretation of the Tetragrammaton, nor to defend the doctrines that have been deduced therefrom. I merely seek to show how the inventors of the Tarot used Qabalistic ideas as the basis for their alphabet of symbols.

The student should understand that the implicits of each letter of the name in the various lists that follow are connected by links of association present in every human mind. The knitting together of apparently unrelated ideas which results from diligent search for, and prolonged meditation upon, these hidden connections, will be found to be one of the principle benefits of this study. In this work a dictionary and a thesaurus will be found useful; but the indispensable feature must be attentive examination of the cards. One might as well try to learn music without singing or playing as to understand to interpret the Tarot without using the pack itself.

As a beginning, let the student trace the connecting links in the following lists of ideas represented by each letter of the name:

Yod

_____

2 EX. 3-15; 1 Kings 10-1; Ps. 9-10; Prov. 18-10.

A hand; creation, executive, realization; Mexican, Hindu, Persian, and Christian symbol of God. In the Zohar, divine royalty, typified by the rod of Moses (Eliphas Levi) ; the active principle of all things (Papus) ; Spirit, Ruach, Prana, or Pneuma, the "life-breath"; inmost principle of man, the Ego, termed Purusha by Hindus.

Heh

A window; suggests (1) admission of light and air into a building, and (2) a means of outlook, which ' enables those within to see what happens outside. The first implicit represents movement from a circumference to a center, or involution; the second stands for motion from within outward, or evolution. Qabalists call Heh "the Mother," and say creation took place therewith. It is a sign of instrumentality, of the universal passive principle, the Non-Ego, which is the Prakriti, or Great Mother, of the Hindus.

Vau

A nail, or hook; fastening, junction, binding, suspension. In the Tetragrammaton, that which joins Yod to Heh. The link between Essence (Purusha) and Substance (Prakriti) i. c., Motion or Force. According to Papus, Vau denotes the universal, passive-active, formative power.

Heh f.

In the Tetragrammaton the second Heh represents the second implicit of the letter-name. It is a sign of evolution, of transmission from one cycle, or plane, of activity to another. Papus compares it to a grain of wheat relatively to the ear, and calls it a Yod in germ-a synthesis of the first three letters, a concentration of their potentialities. It is a sign of Form, which combines Essence, Substance, and Activity.

After digesting the foregoing interpretation of the letters the student will have no trouble to understand the following table:

Yod	Heh	Vau	Heh f.
Spirit	Soul	Astral	Physical body
Archety	Creative	Formativ	Material
Fire	Water	Air	Earth
Lion	Eagle	Man	Bull
Leo^3	Scorpio	Aquarius	Taurus

The implicits of the letters of the name are analogous to the implicits of the first four integers. Yod, as a symbol for the active principle of all things which must be a perfect unity, corresponds to 1. Heh denotes the universal passive principle; that which reflects the One and seems also to antagonize and oppose it. This principle has long been identified with the number 2. Vau, sign

of the union of Yod and Heh (Yod = 10, Heh = 5; Yod + Heh = 10 + 5 = 15 = 1 + 5 = 6, the numerical value of Vau), is analogous to 3, which is the sum of 1 and 2. Finally, as the second Heh is a Yod in germ, so is 4 a potential 1; for by that process of occult mathematics called "theosophic extension" 4=1+2+3+4=10, and by reduction 10--1+0--1.

As a potential 1, the number 4 may be thought of as beginning a second group of integers-4, 5,

6, and 7. In this quaternary, 7 is the second Heh. Thus it is also a Yod in germ. It returns to unity just as 4 does, for it extends to 28=2+8--10. Hence occultists take it as the initial figure of a third quaternary-7, 8, 9, 10. 10 is like 4 and 7. It returns to unity at once, by reduction, and its extension is 5'3=5+5=10--1+0=1.

Perhaps these correspondences cannot be justified by ordinary rules of logic; but, logical or not, they form a recognized part of occult doctrine. As such they are important clues to the. meaning of the Tarot.

They give us, in fact, a key to the general plan of the whole pack. In the minor trumps the correspondences are so obvious that they hardly need to be tabulated; but they are not any more certain than those in the major trumps, though the latter are not so likely to be noticed by a casual observer.

In the minor trumps the Tetragrammaton corresponds to the suits as follows:

---

3 Leo is the fifth sign, Scorpio the eighth, Aquarius the eleventh, and Taurus the second 5+8+11+2 = 26, the sum of the numerical values of the letters of the Tetragrammaton. Mr. Frank C. Higgins, F.R.N.S., is the discoverer of this interesting correspondence.

Yod	Heh	Vau	Heh f.
Wands	Cups	Swords	Pentacles

Its connection with the cards in each suit is:

Yod	Heh	Vau	Heh f.
1	2	3	4
4	5	6	7
7	8	9	10
King	Queen	Knight	Page

The king represents 10, because 10 is Malkuth, "the kingdom", personified by the sovereign.

These four quaternaries stand also in a relation to each other similar to that between the letters of Yod-Heh-Vau-Heh. The first (1, 2, 3, 4) corresponds to Yod, and its members denote activities peculiar to the archetypal world. The second (4, 5, 6, 7) is to the first as Heh is to Yod, and it belongs to the creative world. The activities of the formative world, symbolized by Vau, are indicated by the third group. Finally, the synthesis of all these numbers and planes is the material world, where the abstract powers of the ten Sephiroth, indicated by numbers, assume personal form, represented by the court-cards, which correspond to the second Heh.

The clue to the attribution of Yod-Heh-Vau-Heh to the major trumps is the fact that each letter of the Hebrew alphabet represents a number. From Aleph to Teth the letters are signs for units from 1 to 9; from Yod to Tzaddi they designate tens from 10 to 90, and from Qoph to Tau they stand for hundreds from 100 to 400. Our knowledge of the correspondences between the letters of the Tetragrammaton and numbers, therefore, leads to the following attribution of Yod-Heh- Vau-Heh to the Hebrew alphabet:

Yod	Heh	Vau	Heh final
Aleph 1	Beth 2	Gimel 3	Daleth 4
Daleth 4	Heh 5	Vau 6	Zain 7
Zain 7	Cheth 8	Teth 9	Yod 10
Yod 10	Kaph 20	Lamed	Mem 40
Mem 40	Nun 50	Samekh	Ayin 70
Ayin 70	Peh 80	Tzaddi	Qoph 100
Qoph 100	Resh 200	Shin 300	Tau 400

Substituting the numbers of the major trumps corresponding to the Hebrew letters gives the following table:

	Yod	Heh	Vau	Heh f.

0	1	2	3
3	4	5	6
6	7	8	9
9	10	11	12
12	13	14	15
15	16	17	18
18	19	20	21

The seven quaternaries thus formed are also related to the letters of the name. The first corresponds to Yod, the second to Heh, the third to Vau, and the fourth to the second Heh. This last becomes the Yod of a second series of four quaternaries. Thus, although there are only seven quaternaries in the twenty-two major trumps, they include two distinct groups, of which the first includes the cards from zero to twelve, while the second comprises the trumps from nine to twenty-one. The first group symbolizes the universal process of involution, the descent of spirit into matter, through the four worlds as follows:

	Yod	Heh	Vau	Heh f.	
Yod	0	1	2	3	Archetyp
Heh	3	4	5	6	Creative
Vau	6	7	8	9	Formati
Heh f. 9	10	11	12	Material	

The second series represents the process of evolution, the ascent of spirit from the material to the archetypal plane. Hence the order of the worlds is reversed, thus:

	Yod	Heh	Vau	Heh f.	
Yod	9	10	11	12	Material
Heh	12	13	14	15	Formativ
Vau	15	16	17	18	Creative
Heh f. 18	19	20	21	Archetypal	

In addition to establishing a general meaning for each card in the pack, this arrangement indicates analogies between cards that stand in similar relations to the letters of the Tetragrammaton. There is a marked correspondence between the cards numbered 0, 9,. and 18, for instance, because they are all related to Yod and to the second Heh. The full significance of these correspondences, however, will not be perceived by the student until he has gained some knowledge of the esoteric meaning of the Hebrew alphabet. This will be considered briefly in the next chapter.

CHAPTER III

In the following paragraphs, the first item in bold-face type is the English of the letter-name which heads the paragraph,; the last is the name of the Sephirotic "path" assigned to that letter; the others are Qabalistic correspondences, mostly from the Sepher Yetzirah.[4] Suggestions as to what these attributions imply are printed in ordinary type.

א ALEPH

Ox, or Bull: Apis, Mithra, Dionysos; creative energy, vital principle, solar force.
Ruach: "life breath"; Spiritus, Pneuma, Prana; all-pervading cosmic energy; vital principle of all creatures.
Fiery Intelligence: joins Kether to Chokmah.

ב BETH

House: abode; location; concentration; specialization.
Above: "That which is above" is Purusha, the "superior nature"; Adam.
Mercury: Hermes, Thoth; this planet rules Gemini (Zain) by day, Virgo (Yod) by night.
Life and Death: Specialization implies construction and destruction.
Intelligence of Transparency: joins Kether to Binah.

ג GIMEL

Camel: travel; commerce; intercourse; reciprocal action.
Below: "That which is below" is Prakriti, the subordinate nature; Eve.
The Moon: Artemis, Diana, Hecate; rules Cancer (Cheth) by day and by night. **Peace and Strife**: implied by commerce; symbolized by the bow of Artemis. **Uniting Intelligence**: joins Kether to Tiphareth.

ד
DALETH

Door, or womb: passage; transition; conception; development.
East: "womb of light"; source of illumination; opposite of West (Kaph).
Venus: Aphrodite, Ishtar, the Great Mother; Prakriti, termed "the great

---

4 The planetary attributions are from Book 777, London, 1909.

womb" in the Bhagavad- Gita; rules Libra (Lamed) by day, Taurus (Vau) by night.

Knowledge and Ignorance: as Buddhi, principle of judgment. Prakriti confers knowledge; as Maya, mistress of illusion, she causes ignorance' Illuminating Intelligence: joins Chokmah to Binah.

ה HE

Window: admits light and air; gives outlook.
Sight: vision, contemplation, discernment.
North-East: combines North (Peh) and East (Daleth) ; opposite of South-west (Nun) ; complement of South-cast (Vau).

Aries: diurnal house of Mars (Peh) ; complement of Scorpio (Nun), the nocturnal house. **Constituting Intelligence**: To constitute is to make anything what it is, to frame, to compose; this path joins Chokmah to Tiphareth.

Nail: fastening; union; yoga.

ו VAU

Hearing: unites man to man by speech, and man to Spirit by the Word of the Inner Voice. **South-east**: combines South (Resh) and East (Daleth) ; opposite of North-west (Lamed) ; complement of North-east (Heh).
Taurus: nocturnal house of Venus (Daleth) ; complement of Libra (Lamed), the diurnal house.
Triumphant and Eternal Intelligence: joins Chokmah to Chesed.

ז ZAIN

Sword: opposition; separation; sex.
East-above: combines East (Daleth) and Above (Beth); opposite of West-above (Samekh) ;
complement of East-below (Cheth).
Gemini: diurnal house of Mercury (Beth); complement of Virgo (Yod), the nocturnal house. **Smell**: keen perception, sagacity, discrimination. A Qabalistic aphorism says, "Properties are discerned by the nose."
Disposing Intelligence: joins Chokmah to Tiphareth; to dispose is to place

apart, to separate, to classify.

ח
CHETH

Field: location; that which requires cultivation.
East-below: combines East (Daleth) and Below (Gimel); opposite of West-below (Ayin);
complement of East-above (Zain).
Cancer: diurnal and nocturnal house of the moon (Gimel).
Speech: mastery of language is mastery of thought; the practical occultist devotes much labor to the field of speech.
Intelligence of Influence: joins Binah to Geburah.

ט TETH

Serpent: wisdom, subtlety, secrecy; regeneration; Eliphas Levi's "Astral Light."
Taste: refinement; experience; enduring. patience, fortitude.
North-above: combines North (Peh) and Above (Beth) ; opposite of South-above (Tzaddi) ;
complement of North-below (Yod).
Leo: diurnal and nocturnal house of the sun (Resh).
Intelligence of the Secret: joins Chesed to Geburah.

י Yod

Hand: dexterity, skill; power, might, supremacy; symbol of the Supreme Spirit.
North-below: combines North (Peh) and Below (Gimel); opposite of South-below, (Qoph) ;
complement of North-above (Teth).

Virgo: nocturnal house of Mercury (Beth) ; complement of Gemini (Zain), the diurnal house.
Coition: the union of the male and female, the fixed and the volatile.
Intelligence of Will: joins Chesed to Tiphareth.

כ KAPH

Grasping Hand: control; authority; comprehension; property. **West**: opposite of East (Daleth).
Jupiter: rules Sagittarius (Samekh) by day, and Pisces (Qoph) by night.

Wealth and Poverty: the extremes of "property"; the external signs of one's grasp of circumstances. Intelligence of Conciliation; accommodation of differences; adjustment, establishment of orders; joins Chesed to Netzach.

ל LAMED

Ox--goad: urges and guides the "ox" (Aleph).
Work: action; Karma.
North-west ⁵; combines North (Peh) and West (Kaph); opposite of North-east (Heh);
complement of South-west (Nun).
Libra: diurnal house of Venus (Daleth); complement of Taurus (Van), the nocturnal house.
Faithful Intelligence: joins Geburah to Tiphareth.

ם MEM

Water: "mother, seed, and root of all minerals"; the first mirror; reproduction; reflected life.
Stable Intelligence: "the source of consistency in the numerations"; joins Geburah to Hod.

ן NUN

Fish: compare Joshua, son of Nun, with Jesus (Joshua), whose sign was that of the prophet Jonah. Early Christians called Jesus Ichthys. This also was the name of a son of Aphrodite. **South-west ⁵** : combines South (Resh) and West (Kaph); opposite of North-east (Vau) ;
complement of North-west (Lamed).
Scorpio: nocturnal house of Mars (Peh) ; complement of Aries (Heh),
the diurnal house. Motion: all motion is change.
Imaginative Intelligence: joins Tiphareth to Netzach.

ס
SAMEKH

Prop: support, assistance; improvement, refinement, purification.
West-above: combines West (Kaph) and Above (Beth); opposite of East-above (Zain);
complement of West-below (Ayin).

---

5 Paul Case in 1920 attributed *Lamed to South-West* and *Nun to North-West* but later upon further research, changed these attributions. These have been changed in the text to accord with his later findings. Ed.

Sagittarius: diurnal house of Jupiter (Kaph) ; complement of Pisces (Qoph), the nocturnal house.
Wrath: in Greek, thumos, desire or appetite; akin to the Rajas of Hindu philosophy.

Tentative Intelligence: joins Tiphareth to Yesod.

ע AYIN

Eye: the instrument of vision; orb; circle; limitation; bondage; appearances, Avidya. **Laughter**: usually caused by incongruity; human weaknesses, distress, and pain furnish the elements of comedy.
West-below: combines West (Kaph) and Below (Gimel); opposite of East-below (Cheth) ;
complement of West-above (Samekh).
Capricorn: nocturnal house of Saturn (Tau) ; complement of Aquarius (Tzaddi), the diurnal house. **Renewing Intelligence**: joins Tiphareth to Hod.

פ Peh

Mouth: organ of speech; out of it are the issues of life.
North: darkness, cold, sterility; place of the sun's annual death; opposite of South (Resh).
Mars: rules Aries (Heh) by day, and Scorpio (Nun) by night. Grace and Indignation: contrasting expressions of the fiery power of Mars.
Exciting Intelligence: joins Netzach to Hod.

צ
TZADDI

Fish-hook: that which pulls the fish (Nun) out of water (Mem); to hook is to draw, entice, procure by artifice.
South-above: combines South (Resh) and Above (Beth); opposite of North-above (Teth); complement of South-below (Qoph).
Aquarius: diurnal house of Saturn (Tau); complement of Capricorn (Ayin), the nocturnal house. **Meditation**: Dhyana, "an unbroken flow of knowledge in a particular object"; a diving into the depths of the mind for ideas-a fishing for truth.
Natural Intelligence: joins Netzach to Yesod.

ק

QOPH

Back of head, or knot: location of medulla oblongata, which forms a knot on the spinal cord

near the nape of the neck. It controls or greatly influences many functions which make it directly responsible for the maintenance of bodily life.

South-below: combines South (Resh) and Below (Gimel); opposite of North-below (Yod) ; complement of South-above (Tzaddi).

Sleep: period of physiological repair, during which nerve substance undergoes the subtle changes that make the advancing student of occultism ready to experience and understand facts, concealed from ordinary men, which are the basis of the ancient wisdom.

Pisces: nocturnal house of Jupiter (Kaph) ; complement of Sagittarius (Samekh), the diurnal

house. **Corporeal Intelligence**: joins Netzach to Malkuth.

ר RESH

Head, or face: guiding power, organizer, director; the face is the countenance, from the Latin continere, to hold together, to repress, to contain.

South: place of sun at his meridian height; opposite of North (Peh). Sun: rules Leo (Teth) day and night.

Fruitfulness and Sterility: extremes of the manifestation of solar energy. The sun causes all

growth, and is also the maker of waste places.

Collecting Intelligence: joins Hod to Yesod. Note the correspondence between collecting and countenance.

ש SHIN

Tooth: probably serpent's fang; sharpness; acidity; active manifestation of the fire-principle.

Fire: the Spirit of God is a "consuming fire"; in Hebrew that Spirit is Ruach Elohim and the letters of these two words represent the numbers 200, 6, 8, 1, 30, 5, 10

and 40, giving a total of 300. This is the value of Shin, the sound of which suggests the hissing of fire.

Perpetual Intelligence: joins Hod to Malkuth.

ת
TAU

Cross: the Egyptian Tau was a tally for measuring the depth of the Nile, also a square for measuring right angles; among the Hebrews it was a sign of salvation (Ezek. ix. 4) ; in Freemasonry it is a "symbol of salvation from death, and of eternal life."[6]

The palace of holiness in the midst, sustaining all things: the' "heavenly city"; the "temple"; a structure complete, whole and perfect, built four-square by the Master-Builder.

Saturn: he who swallows his children; that which absorbs all things into itself; rules Aquarius (Tzaddi) by day, and Capricorn (Ayin) by night.

Power and Servitude: service is the secret of power; he who would rule Nature must obey her laws.

Administrative Intelligence: joins Yesod to Malkuth.

Memorize these attributions. Develop the implicits by your own research and meditation. Remember that the object of Tarot study is to bring up from the depths of the mind ideas common to all men, which, in the past, have been expressed only by the few, but are now being recognized by increasing numbers of people. The Qabalistic meanings of the Hebrew alphabet may be likened to seeds, having within them the whole potency of the Secret Doctrine, however little they may resemble that doctrine itself. Make them your own. Give special attention to the correspondences between letters representing directions, sins, and planets. Not until you have mastered every point of this outline will you be ready to study the occult significance of numbers, which you will be asked to consider in the next chapter.

---

6 Mackey "Encyclopedia of Freemasonry." p. 791.

CHAPTER IV

No very extensive knowledge of occult mathematics is required by beginners in Tarot-study. All that is absolutely necessary may be stated in a few paragraphs. It is developed from the
Qabalistic doctrine of a ten-fold emanation from the Absolute.

The Absolute is Ain Suph, No Limit. From Kapila and the Bhavagad Gita to Spinoza and Sir William Hamilton, philosophers always describe it by negatives. Boehme, for example, says: "It may fitly be compared to Nothing, for it is deeper than anything, and is as nothing with respect to all things." The idea of depth emphasized by Boehme echoes Lao-tze, who calls the Absolute "the Mother-deep." This feminine aspect of the Absolute is recognized by all deep thinkers, for that in which lies the potentiality of all things must be as truly Mother as Father. This feminine potency is represented by the zero-sign, 0, a circle or oval, symbol of the Great Mother and of the egg of the universe. The Changeless 0, which cannot be added to, subtracted from, multiplied, nor divided, is a perfect numerical symbol for Ain. Suph. In the major trumps of the Tarot it is represented by The Fool.

The initial emanation from Ain Suph is Kether, the Crown, identical with the Supernal Source in all but name, the Creative Principle in the beginning. The inherent mental quality of the Supernal Originating Principle is implied through the Qabalah. Its primary expression, therefore, cannot be other than some form of Will; and the first conceivable manifestation of that Will in beginning the creative process would be the selection of a particular point in space at which to start. Hence Qabalists call Kether the Primal Will, and sometimes refer to it as the "Small Point." The point corresponds geometrically to 1, which represents what Eliphas Levi terms "the relative unity, manifested, possessing duality, the beginning of numerical sequence." The student should note particularly that the number 1 possesses duality. This idea is a key to many occult truths.

The duad is Chokmah,[7] Wisdom. the number of science, since all scientific

---

[7] The aspect of Chokmah represented in the Tarot by the number 2, and the High Priestess, is the Lesser Chokmah mentioned in the twenty--first chapter of the Lesser Holy, Assembly,. It is female in respect to Kether.

knowledge is based upon comparison; of Woman as the wife of Man., of antagonism, opposition, and polarity; and also of equilibrium. The duad is the especial symbol of Memory, because every recollection duplicates an original experience. Perfect memory is required to continue a creative process springing from a Limitless Absolute and begun by an Infinite Will; and this perfect recollection of every stage of development is the essence of that Wisdom by which, says the Bible, the Lord founded the earth. Whosoever can understand the saying, "God creates by remembering Himself," is very near to the real meaning of the duad. He will understand, moreover, why the full significance of this number must be concealed from the profane.

The triad is Binah (BINH), Understanding, which, says The Lesser Holy Assembly, "comprehendeth all things. . . . For in the word BINH are shown Father, Mother, and Son; since by the letters IH Father and Mother are denoted, and the letters BN, denoting the Son are amalgamated with them." Binah is the Great Sea, Mare-Mary the Great Mother. Her ancient symbol is an equilateral triangle with the apex turned downward-the Phoenician character for the letter Daleth. Papus says: The hieroglyphic meaning of Daleth is the womb. It suggests an object giving plentiful nourishment, the source of future growth." By gematria, BINH = 2+10+50+5 = 67 = 13 = 4, and the value of Daleth is 4. Again, since BINH = 67=13, it suggests the self-division of the One which is the foundation of the creative process, for the Name of the One is IHVH = 26, and 13 (BINH) =26 --'2, or IHVH divided by Chokmah (2). Finally, in the Tarot Daleth is The Empress, who corresponds to the number 3. This number denotes extension, expansion, increase, growth, and generative activity.

In some respects, Chesed, the fourth Sephirah, is a repetition of Kether, because its number, 4, is
10 by extension (1 +2+3+4), and the reduction of 10 (1+0) is 1. As Kether is "The Crown," so is Chesed sometimes called Gedulah,, or "Majesty." Mercy, or Benevolence, the self-imparting aspect of the Primal Will, is the fundamental meaning of this number, which the Tarot
symbolizes by The Emperor.

Geburah, Strength or Severity, also named justice (Din), or Fear (Pechad), is the Sephirah corresponding to the number 5. This number is the mean term between 1, the beginning of the integral series, and 9, its end. Hence it implies balance, or equilibrium. That this is the root- quality of justice needs

23

no demonstration. Equilibrium, moreover, is the Great Arcanum of magic,. The search for it entails trials of the utmost rigor and severity trials which inspire the unprepared with chilling fear., but when they are passed, the seeker finds in balance an exhaustless source of strength. Therefore, in the Tarot is this number and Sephirah represented by The Hierophant, the "revealer of the mysteries" of the Great Arcanum.

From 5 proceeds 6, for the extension of 5 is 15, and by reduction 15 is 6. This number also proceeds directly from 3 by extension; and as 3 is itself the extension of 2, the number 6 is really involved in, or implied by, the duad. Of this its geometrical symbol is a reminder, for the hexagram, or six-pointed star, is composed of two interlaced equilateral triangles, a double triad. This is what Eliphas Levi means when he says that in a certain aspect "the senary is only the duad exalted and carried to its extreme power." The corresponding Sephirah is Tiphareth, Beauty; and as all true beauty implies rhythm, harmony, and symmetry, it is not difficult to understand why the hexagram, the geometrical basis of the snow-flake, is regarded by Qabalists as its most appropriate symbol. There Are other, and deeper, correspondences, moreover, between the number 6 and the idea of Beauty. Upon these I hope to be able to dwell at greater length when I come to the interpretation of the sixth major trump, The Lovers.

The union of 1 and 6 produces 7, which in this aspect is a symbol of the harmonious manifestation of the specializing power represented by 1. But it is as the sum of 3 and 4, represented by the figure of an equilateral triangle surmounting a square, that the septenary reveals its deepest meaning. As the sum of the triad and the tetrad, 7 is the sacred number of all religions, and, especially, a summary of the whole secret doctrine of Israel. It corresponds to the Sephirah Netzach, Victory, and is represented in the major trumps by The Chariot.

The number 8 is that of the Sephirah Hod, Eternal Order, or Splendor. Eliphas Levi says: "It represents motion, Yet also, and more than all, stability; it reconciles the opposed laws of nature. explains eternity by time, faith by knowledge, God by man. It is the number of eternal life, which is maintained by the equilibrium of motion." This is the only cube among the integers, formed by the double multiplication of the duad (2 x 2 x 2). Here' for discerning students, is an important clue to the occult significance of 8. Another is that by its extension it produces 36, a number representing the combination of the triad and the senary or Understanding and Beauty. Finally, the Sephirah Hod is the seat of "The Intelligence of the Secret," and the secret is that of the direction of the Great Magical Agent. Even the shape of the figure 8 is a hint of that secret. Far more than a hint is given in the symbolism of the eighth major trump in Mr. Waite's pack, entitled Strength.

In 8, because its extension is 36--3+6=9, is concealed the potency of 9, and the nature of that potency is revealed by the fact that in the symbolism of number 9 stands for prophecy and initiation. In occult mathematics, therefore, initiation and prophecy are considered to be manifestations of the power of the duad, because they are expressed by a number which results from the extension of the cube of the duad. That they are so in fact is understood by every occultist who has mastered even the rudiments of the Sacred Science. As the final term of the integral series, 9 signifies completion. Hence it is a symbol of perfection, entirety, and realization; and it denotes those who have reached the heights of attainment-the experts, virtuosi, adepts, and illuminati. It is the number of Yesod, the Sephirah of Foundation, the scat of "Pure Intelligence." In the Tarot it corresponds to The Hermit.

As the last of the integers, the number 9 really completes the series of simple mathematical ideas from which all others are derived; but in the scheme of the Sephiroth the number 10 is included. It is assigned to Malkuth, the Kingdom, declared by Qabalists to be the Shekinah, or divine halo which encircles all the other nine Sephiroth, and encompasses the whole in its presence. The number 10 represents the combination of the Manifest (1) and the Unmanifest (0), the particular and the universal, the Primal Will (Kether) and the Limitless Absolute (Ain Suph). It is a sign of the totality of existence, of the perfection and consummation of all things. As the extension of 4, it is the sum of the monad, the duad, the triad, and the tetrad, and so combines all the fundamental mathematical conceptions of the Sacred Science. It is also produced by the reduction of the extension of 7 (28 =2+8 =10). Finally, it is the number which brings all the integers back to unity, since 10 =1+0 =1 ; and its own extension, 55, is not only the double pentad, but is also significant of the eternal self-reproduction of the Divine Kingdom, since 55=5+5=10. Its representative in the major trumps is The Wheel of Fortune.

The student who has read, in Chapter 1, that the twenty-two major trumps correspond to the twenty-two letters of the Hebrew alphabet, may wonder why I am now assigning them to the Sephiroth. The reason is that each trump has a double significance. For the paths between the Sephiroth, indicated by the twenty-two letters, are really only forms or stages of the activity of the Sephiroth themselves. And the student will find, as he progresses in his study of the cards, that whatever apparent confusion may arise from the fact that each trump has two meanings will disappear when the full extent of each meaning is grasped, simply because the two are really aspects of a single truth.

In conclusion, let me give a simple rule for determining the Sephirotic correspondence of any major trump bearing a number higher than 10. First, reduce the number to an integer; second, find the extension of that integer, and reduce it also.

Example:

What is the Sephirotic value of trump 17, The Star ?

17==1+7= 8, therefore The Star represents an aspect of Splendor, the eighth Sephirah, and should be compared, for study, with Strength.

The extension of 8 is 36. This may be articulated as 3 and 6, hence we know that The Star represents, in the extension, or development, of the power symbolized by it, a combination of the principles represented by The Empress and The Lovers, or the Sephiroth Binah and Tiphareth.

The reduction of 36 is 9. Hence we may study The Hermit for a symbolic presentation of the secret doctrine about what results from the development of the activity represented by The Star.

These considerations, combined with what we shall learn of each card by the analysis of its symbolism in connection with the secret meaning of the Hebrew letter to which it corresponds, will enable us to establish our study of the Tarot upon a sure foundation. In succeeding chapters I shall endeavour to furnish outlines for such study.

CHAPTER V

In the Tarot the archetypal triad of involution is represented by the Fool, the Magician, and the High Priestess. Readers who possess the cards can better follow the explanation of the symbols if they will place these three trumps on a table, with the Magician immediately below the Fool,
and the left upper corner of the next card just touching the right lower corner of the picture of the Magician, so that his left hand will be pointing toward the black pillar on the High Priestess' right. In this arrangement, the Fool stands in the place of Ain Suph, and the Magician and High Priestess indicate the positions of Kether and Chokmah on the Qabalistic "Tree of Life."

The Fool is Yod of Yod, the archetypal active principle of involution before manifestation, not as It really is, because the Absolute transcends finite comprehension, but as It has revealed Itself, in a measure, to the wise. He is Ain, No-thing, Ain Suph, No Limit, and Ain Suph Aur, Limitless Light. This last designation is the keynote of occult doctrine. What it implies is confirmed by the discoveries of modern scientists, although they approach Truth by other paths than those of occultism.

Because we must think of the Absolute in terms of our own experience, It presents Itself to us in human form (The Fool); but behind this personal seeming the sages discern something higher- typified in this picture by the white sun-an Impersonal Power, manifesting as the Limitless Energy radiated to the planets of innumerable world systems by their suns. In manifestation, that Energy, symbolized also by the fair hair of the traveler, is temporarily limited by living organisms. Of these the vegetable kingdom, represented by the green wreath, is the primary
class, from which, in course of evolution, spring animal organisms, typified by the red feather. The Supreme Spirit is forever young, forever in the morning of its power, forever on the verge of the abyss of manifestation. It always faces unknown possibilities of self-expression transcending any height it may have reached at a given time; hence the Fool faces west, toward a peak above and beyond his present station. It is THAT which was, is, and shall be, and this is indicated by the Hebrew letters Yod-Heh-Vau-Heh, faintly traced on the collar of the Fool's under garment. This inner robe is the dazzling white Light of Perfect Wisdom (Sattva, in Hindu

philosophy) ; and it is concealed by the black coat of Ignorance (Tamas), lined with the red of passion, fire, and material force (Rajas). This outer garment is embroidered with what seems to be a floral decoration, but the unit of design is a solar orb, containing a red double solar cross, surrounded by seven triple flames. These are the seven Spirits of God, the Elohim, through whose activity all forms are projected, according to laws analogous to those of the vegetable kingdom.

The primary manifestation of Spirit is Will, of which Attention-the wand-is the essence, and to which Memory-the wallet-is closely linked. Wisdom, having for its essence Imagination-the rose-is the secondary expression. Upon the progress of this vital principle in humanity depends the advancement of the sub-human forms, represented by the dog.

A key to the true significance of the title is the saying, "The wisdom of God is foolishness with men." The name of this trump also indicates the folly of every attempt to define the Supreme Spirit. All names are definitions, and to define God is to blaspheme Him.

As Heh of Yod, the Magician is passive to Ain Suph, hence he is a symbolic antithesis to the Fool. He is God the Creator in the Beginning, in contrast to God the Principle before all beginnings. He is Kether, the Primal Will which initiates the creative process by selecting a particular point in space at which to begin.

His passive relation to Ain Suph Aur, Limitless Light, is indicated by his uplifted right hand, holding the magic wand by means of which he draws down power from above. That power is the descending Energy typified by the Fool; and the Magician's wand, in the arrangement of the cards explained at the beginning of this chapter, points directly to the verge of the abyss whereon the traveler is poised.

The Magician's left hand points toward the High Priestess. It is as if he were the medium through which the Limitless Light finds expression in Chokmah. This gesture also denotes concentration, and the selective action of Creative Will. The same selective action is also suggested by the table, which implies definite location, and is, in one sense, a symbol of the material universe. The emblems of the Tarot suits lying upon it are the elements used by the Magician in his work.

28

Roses above his head and at his feet suggest the Hermetic axiom, "That which is above is as that which is below." The Magician himself, moreover, through his correspondence to Beth, corresponds to the direction Above, which indicates that lie is "the superior nature" or Purusha of Hindu philosophers. He is the Onlooker, the objective aspect of Infinite Intelligence, perceiving nature as something other than himself. In Egyptian mythology he is Thoth, in the mysteries of Greece he is Hermes, and in the allegory of Genesis he is Adam, the first man, or first mode of mind.

The roses in the garden are symbols of the universal feminine principle, and they grow side by side with lilies, which are masculine emblems. Thus the flowers, which belong to the Magician, and which he cultivates, remind us of the doctrine that the number One possesses duality : for they denote the Law of Gender, an important aspect of the duad.

Over the Magician's head is the lemniscate symbol of the Holy Spirit. A double zero, it represents the ancient doctrine that in creating Spirit divides itself, so that the One becomes Two. The central point of contact is Kether, the "Small Point" of primary manifestation.

Because even the Primal Will is a limitation of Ain Suph, it possesses some degree of the quality of darkness. Hence the Magician's hair is black; but a golden band surrounds it, to show that the Darkness is held in cheek by Light. Here is the antithesis to the Fool's yellow hair and his green wreath.

The Magician's red mantle symbolizes Light and Creative Force (Rajas); his white robe denotes Purity and Wisdom (Sattva); and his blue serpent girdle represents Time and Occult Science, because the Ancient Wisdom is the fruit of observations and experiments begun thousands of years ago.

The High Priestess is the archetypal formative principle, Vau of Yod, which combines the potency of the Originating Yod (The Fool) with the initiative and selection of the Creative Heh (The Magician). The Fool may be represented as a circle, the Magician as the center, and the High Priestess as the diameter, dividing the circle into two equal parts. The circle is Infinite Intelligence; the center is the Primal Will, and the extension of that Will toward the limitless circumference is the Line, the geometrical correspondence to the number Two. This is Chokmah, the

Sephirah of Perfect Wisdom. The High Priestess is the feminine Chokmah, personified in proverbs as a woman, passive in her relation to Kether.

Literally, her name means "The Superior Feminine Elder," or the archetypal feminine principle. She is what Hindus call Prakriti, the inferior nature of the Supreme Spirit. Yet she is one in essence with the superior nature, Purusha, from which she proceeds. The Emerald Table of Hermes says the same thing, "As above, so below;" and the bearing of this upon Qabalistic doctrine in the Tarot is the fact that the Sepher Yetzirah attributes to Beth (The Magician) the direction "Above," and to Gimel (the High Priestess) the direction "Below." She is Eve, before her union with Adam; and she also wears the horned crown and blue robe of Isis. The color of her vestments likewise connects her with the Virgin Mary, and the moon at her feet suggests the goddess Artemis, or Diana, also a virgin.

In more than sex is she the antithesis of the Magician. His mantle represents Fire and Light; her garments, in both color and line, remind us of Cold and Moisture. The Magician stands; but she sits on a cubic stone, a symbol of Salt, which crystallizes in perfect cubes, and a reminder of the saltness of that mystic Sea which is associated with the name of Mary. The Magician is out-of- doors; but the High Priestess sits in a temple. He is the objective aspect of consciousness, the Cognizer of the universe and its laws; she is the subjective aspect, reflecting what he perceives, and recording it upon the scroll of the Memory of Nature. That scroll is inscribed with the word TORA, the four letters of which, arranged in certain ways, afford a clue to the whole mystery of the Tarot. As written on the scroll, they are the phonetic equivalent of the Hebrew *Torah*, the Law.

The pillars are those of Solomon and Hermes. Opposite in color, but alike in form, they represent Affirmation ("J" or Jachin) and Negation ("B" or Boaz). For strength (Boaz) is rooted in resistance, or inertia - the negation of the Establishing Principle (Jachin) of all things. The High Priestess sits between the pillars, because she is the equilibrating principle between the "Yes" and the "No," the initiative and the resistance, the Light and the Darkness.

From the pillars hangs a veil, embroidered with palms and pomegranates. The palms are masculine emblems, and the pomegranates are feminine. The latter are so disposed upon the veil, that, although but seven can be seen, three more would be shown were not the High Priestess in the way. The basis of this design is the Qabalistic "Tree of Life." Qabalists will notice that the crown of the High Priestess has its horns in Chokmah ,and Binah, and its orb in Daath (Knowledge). The lower point of the solar cross on her breast touches Tiphareth; and her seat, the Cubic Stone of Salt and of the Material Universe, is in Yesod, the Foundation, and Malkuth, the Kingdom. Lack of space forbids a more extended explanation of this arrangement; but the keys to it are already in the possession of readers who have mastered the elements of the preceding chapters, and it will be even more intelligible as we proceed with the interpretation of the other major trumps.

Such is an outline of the significance of the first triad. Let the student ponder upon it, and amplify it for himself. To each person some aspects of the doctrine of the Tarot are more obvious than others. Yet they are all related, and he who masters these first principles may be sure that, in due time, he will find them leading him to other, and higher aspects of that One Truth that is back of them all.

CHAPTER VI

Arrange the major trumps from 0 to 5 as

follows:

$$
\begin{array}{cc}
& 0 \\
& 1 \\
3 & 2 \\
5 & 4 \\
\end{array}
$$

The Empress will then be in *Binah,* the Emperor in *Chesed,* and the Hierophant in *Geburah,* on the Tree of Life. As final *Heh* of the archetypal world, the Empress is a synthesis of 0, 1, and 2. Her yellow hair, bound by a green wreath, repeats the symbolism of the Fool; her uplifted sceptre resembles the Magician's wand; and, like the High Priestess, she is a woman, seated on a cubic stone. As *Yod* of *Heh,* she is both the reflection and the antithesis of the Fool. He is a youth, standing on a barren height: she is a matron, sitting in the midst of a fertile valley.

She is *Binah,* Understanding, the Sanctifying Intelligence, termed "the foundation of Primordial Wisdom," because Divine Wisdom proceeds from that perfect understanding of Itself and of Its power through which Spirit purifies and completes all its creations. This purifying power is associated with Water (represented by a stream and pool in the background of the picture), and *Binah,* as the "root of Water," corresponds to the Great Sea – Prakriti, Aphrodite, Mare – Mary. She is also the Salt which **is** the active principle of that Sea.

In Chapter IV I have shown how the word BINH, through its number, 67, which reduces to 13, symbolizes the apparent self-division of Spirit. The opposite aspect of the creative process is indicated by another name for the third Sephirah – AIMA, "the bright pregnant Mother" – which refers to those characteristics of *Binah* emphasized by the symbolism of the Empress. AIMA is
1, 10, 40, 1, or *52* – the *doubling* of 26 (IHVH), and the sum of the values of the letters of the Tetragrammaton spelt in full (IUD- HH - VV - HH: 10, 6, 4; *5, 5; 6, 6; 5, 5).* It signifies the multiplication of the Supreme Spirit (IHVH: 26) by Wisdom *(Chokmah: 2).* Fifty-two is also the value of the word BN, *Ben,* the Son, associated by Qabalists with *Tiphareth,* the sixth Sephirah;

and the reduction of *52* gives 7, the number of the letter *Zain,* corresponding to the major trump of the Lovers, which bears the number 6, and represents *Tiphareth* by its emblems. In AIMA, the Mother, BN, the Son, **is** concealed, even as the Son **is** comprehended, together with the Father (I), and the Mother (H), in BINH. Even so in the number 3, assigned to the Empress, is concealed the number 6, for 6 is the extension of 3.

As the "root of Water" *Binah* corresponds to *Daleth,* because the alchemical symbol of Water, an equilateral triangle pointing downward, was the ancient Semitic character for *Daleth.* Furthermore, the value of *Daleth* is 4, the final reduction of 67, the number of the word BINH. Nor are these the only links between the Sephirah and the letter, for to *Daleth* is attributed the planet Venus, or Aphrodite. The symbol of Venus appears on the heart-shaped shield beside the Empress, and a variation of it is embroidered upon her robe. The Empress' crown of twelve stars represents the zodiac, the year, and so Time. It corresponds to the girdle of the Fool, which has twelve jewels. It also denotes the *Shemahamphorash,* or seventy-two explanatory names of God, for the stars are six pointed, and 12 x 6 is 72. For Qabalists this should be especially significant.

As creative *Heh* the Emperor is the antithesis of the Magician. The latter, young, dark-haired and beardless, stands in a garden; the Emperor, white-haired and bearded, sits on a throne of granite, in a desert place. Rugged mountain-peaks tower behind him in the distance. At their base flows a river.

Heh is *Chesed,* Mercy or Beneficence; but he corresponds particularly to the aspect of *Chesed* termed GEDULAH, Majesty. In a sense he is the crown of the Empress, because the number of *Chesed is 72.* Her power is derived from, and subordinate to his, for he is merely another aspect of the same principle represented by the Magician; but because the feminine principle predominates in the creative world, he is to her as *Heh* to *Yod.*

The name of the Path assigned to *Gedulah* suggests the same thought of passivity. It is the Measuring Intelligence, which "arises like a boundary to receive the emanations of the higher intelligences which are set down to it. Herefrom all spiritual virtues emanate by the way of subtlety, which itself emanates from the Supreme Crown." These phrases of medieval Qabalism convey the same idea of self-impartation that is implied by "Beneficence," and intimate that this free gift of Its powers is part of the very essence of the Primal Will.

In Mr. Waite's Tarot, the symbolism of the Emperor emphasizes his correspondence to *Heh* in the alphabet. Ram's heads, representing Aries, adorn his throne. Another is embroidered on his cape. Straight lines drawn from the apex of his crown to his hands, and from hand to hand, will form the upright triangle of Fire; and Aries is a Fire sign.

Beneath a red robe, like the Magician's, he wears armor. This connects him with Mars, which rules Aries by day, because iron is the metal attributed to Mars. In the major trumps Mars is represented by the Tower, which is 16, or 4 x 4. Again, the Sun, which is exalted in Aries, is 19 in the major trumps, and the first reduction of 19 is 10, which is the extension of 4. I have no space to explain these correspondences; but l call attention to them so that earnest students may work out the doctrines implied for themselves.

The Emperor's crown has twelve divisions. Five (the number of *Heh)* are visible. Surmounting it are three small circles, arranged to form an inverted triangle, to remind us that *Chesed* corresponds to the element Water. Note the distinction between *Binah,* the "root of Water," and *Chesed,* to which Water itself is attributed.

In a sense, too, the Emperor reflects the High Priestess, beneath whom he stands on the Tree of Life. His number is the square of hers, and his power is, in one aspect, the duplication of hers. In addition to his red robe and his armor, therefore, he wears another garment, blue, like her robe.

His sceptre is a Tau-cross (see explanation of *Tau* in Chapter III), surmounted by a sun wheel. It denotes the mastery and direction of Fire by the use of an instrument designed to measure Water. He is the same combination of Fire and Water that is implied by the fact that the Emperor symbolizes both *Chesed* and Aries. The sceptre also implies that the Extension of Light in creative activity is according to laws of mathematics. To practical occultists it should, moreover, convey a very definite hint of the means to be employed in directing the Universal Fire. *Verbum sap.*

The Hierophant, "revealer of sacred mysteries," is *Vau* of the creative world – the link between the Emperor and the Empress. He is also the reflection and the antithesis of the High Priestess, who is the archetypal *Vau.*

As 1 plus 4, his number combines those of the Magician and the Emperor. The two kneeling ministers, therefore, have the lilies and roses of the Magician embroidered on their robes; and the Hierophant's position of authority, indicated by his throne, tiara, and sceptre, reflects the idea of rulership suggested by the Emperor.

The number 5 is also 2 plus 3. The name of the Hierophant is the masculine equivalent of "High Priestess"; he sits in a building, between two pillars; and one of his vestments is blue. His correspondence to the Empress is shown by his white undergarment, by the three bars of his sceptre, and by the white *pallium* which he wears over his red robe. This last is a circle surmounting a vertical line, double the diameter of the circle. The line, therefore, is equal to the two lines forming the cross in the symbol of Venus, of which the *pallium* is really a variant. The sign which the Hierophant makes with his right hand signifies, "Two concealed and Three revealed," or the manifestation of the hidden duad (the High Priestess), through the activity of the triad (the Empress). Again, the extension of 5 is 15; and this reduces to 6, the extension of 3, which, in turn, is the extension of 2. Finally, the number 5 corresponds to the number 2 in the "quaternary numeration" based on the correspondence of numbers to the letters of IHVH, as explained in an earlier chapter.

As a symbol for *Geburah,* Strength or Severity, the Hierophant is the Radical Intelligence which "emanates from the depths of the Primordial Wisdom." That Wisdom is *Chokmah* (the High Priestess), and the Hierophant represents its creative manifestation. By this is he connected with the Great Arcanum of the Pentagram as it is explained in the writings of Eliphas Levi.

His correspondence to *Vau* in the alphabet makes him a symbol of the Triumphant and Eternal Intelligence which is the Path joining *Chokmah* (2: the High Priestess) to *Chesed* (4: the Emperor). He also corresponds to the zodiacal sign Taurus, the first of the Earth triplicity. Taurus is the nocturnal house of Venus (the Empress), and the exaltation of the Moon (the High Priestess).

Consult the data given in preceding chapters for other meanings of this triad of trumps, and devote a little time each day to tracing out the connections. Keep a note-book for each major trump, with main headings like those I have used in explaining the Hebrew alphabet, and other headings for the ideas suggested by the title, number, and symbols of the card.

By following this plan you will quickly accumulate much information, classified in such a way that you can refer to it easily. Remember that, apart from its general doctrine, the Tarot has a special message for you, because it speaks by evoking thought. Record what it tells you in the manner just explained, and you will understand why adepts, for generations, have counted this book of symbols among their most cherished possessions.

CHAPTER VII

To the tableau of major trumps previously given, add 6, 7, and 8, as follows:

$$0$$
$$1$$
$$3 \quad 2$$
$$5 \quad 4$$
$$6$$
$$8 \quad 7$$

The Lovers will then be in *Tiphareth,* the Chariot in *Netzach,* and Strength in *Hod.*

As final *Heh* of the creative quaternary, the Lovers is a synthesis of 3, 4, and 5. The woman **is** the Empress, the man the Emperor, and the angel the Hierophant. The man and woman also correspond to the two ministers of the Hierophant, to the pillars of the High Priestess, and to the lilies and roses of the Magician. The man, again, symbolizes the masculine pillar of the Tree of Life *(Chokmah, Chesed, and Netzach),* and the woman typifies the feminine pillar *(Binah, Geburah, and Hod).* The angel between them is the middle pillar *(Kether, Tiphareth, Yesod, and Malkuth).*

As *Yod* of *Vav,* the sixth trump symbolizes the active principle of the formative world. That principle is RVCh, *Ruach,* the Life-Breath, ascribed by Qabalists to *Tiphareth,* to which they also assign the Sun and the angel Michael. In the Lovers, the Sun is at the top of the picture, and Michael, riding on a cloud, which typifies the atmosphere, blesses the scene below. The symbolism may be interpreted thus: The Universal Energy, concentrated in the Sun, and modified by the atmosphere, is the formative principle of all things.

That Energy works through a law which produces the phenomena of sex in living organism. The root of this law is the self-division of Spirit. By that self-division, or self-reflection, the One becomes Two, the One and Two unite to form Three, and from the extension of Three proceeds Six. In the Lovers, the man is One, the Magician (Adam), and the woman is Two, the High Priestess (Eve). The angel corresponds to the Fool.

37

This reading of the symbols differs from that given in the second paragraph, but the difference is only apparent; for the lilies and roses of the Magician are emblems of his power and that of the High Priestess, and the pillars between which she sits are, in one sense, herself and the Magician. She is the equilibrating power between the black pillar (feminine) and the white pillar (masculine). The idea behind all this apparent confusion of symbols is this: Spirit manifests itself through the activity of its own Power, and by that Power (Prakriti, the High Priestess) regulates itself. In some phases of manifestation the female aspect of Spirit is emphasized, and appears to be the controlling principle; in other phases the masculine aspect is the more prominent; and there are still other modes of self-expression wherein the masculine and feminine both seem to be subordinate to a higher aspect, which transcends distinctions of gender.

Besides the implicits suggested by the correspondence of the Lovers to the various Qabalistic meanings of *Zain,* the student should observe that *Zain* represents Ruach, because RVCh is the number 214, which reduces to 7, or *Zain.* This is another link between the Lovers and *Tiphareth,* wherein *Ruach* is especially active. It likewise indicates a correspondence between the Lovers
and the Fool, who corresponds to *Ruach* through *Aleph.* The number 7, furthermore, is analogous
to 1, the number of *Aleph,* because 28, the extension of 7, has 1 for its final reduction. So, too, *Zain,* corresponds to *Daleth,* for *Daleth* is 4, which extends to 10. Finally the number of the Lovers (VI) is the extension of that of the Empress (III).

In direct antithesis to the Lovers, yet repeating much of their symbolism, is the Chariot, *Heh* of the formative world. The Charioteer is the angel of the Sun, but he has descended into the cubic chariot of Matter. This is drawn by sphinxes, corresponding to the man and woman, and to the pillars of the High Priestess. The Lovers stand in a garden, but the Chariot is on a plain, before a walled city. Behind it is a river, like that which rises in the garden of the Empress and flows through the valley behind the Emperor.

The Chariot is *Netzach,* Victory, the seat of Occult Intelligence. To this Sephirah Qabalists ascribe the element Fire, and lines drawn from the Charioteer's hands to his crown, and from hand to hand, form the upright triangle of Fire. This rests on the square face of the Chariot, so that the complete figure is a triangle surmounting a square. It symbolizes the number Seven (3 plus 4) and also the union of Spirit and Matter. The square may also be represented by a cross, and then the Charioteer in his car typifies the alchemical Sulphur, analogous to the *Rajas* of Hindu philosophers.

To the implicits of *Cheth,* the letter corresponding to the Chariot, the following observations may be added:

1. The letter-name *Cheth,* ChITh, is 418, which gives 13 (a number that we recognize as a symbol of BINH) and 4 *(Daleth,* the Empress), by reduction. The river behind the Charioteer,
and his fair hair, bound by a green wreath, repeat the symbolism of the Empress, who is BINH. She is the "Root of Water," and Cancer, the first sign of the Water triplicity, is assigned to *Cheth.*
2. In Cancer the Moon rules day and night. This is indicated by the crescents on the Charioteer's shoulders. The Moon is the High Priestess, whose pillars correspond to the sphinxes that draw the Chariot. She is *Gimel,* GML, 73, which reduces to 10, and 10 is the extension of 4, the reduction of the value of ChITh.
3. The number of *Cheth,* the letter, is 8, the cube of 2, and 2 is *Beth,* the Magician, whose wand corresponds to the scepter of the Charioteer. 8, moreover, is the reduction, of IHVH 26,
and of IShVO, 386 (the Aramaic form of the name *Jesus).* In symbolism, 8 is commonly represented by an eight-armed cross, an emblem that has been employed in every age and clime to designate the Sun. The eight-pointed star on the Charioteer's crown has the same meaning.

These are only a few of the implicits suggested by the Chariot, but lack of space obliges me to leave further development of the interpretation to the student, who should note that the number of the Chariot (VII) establishes its correspondence to the Magician (I), to the Emperor (IV), and to the Wheel of Fortune (X). This last is a symbol of Jupiter, the planet exalted in Cancer.

In the zodiac, Cancer is followed by Leo, attributed to the letter *Teth,* and represented in the
Tarot by Strength. In one respect older versions of this picture are better than Mr. Waite's. In the latter a woman closes a lion's mouth, but in the older

symbolism the mouth of the lion is opened by his mistress. The woman is *Binah,* and the lion is the Astral Light. To "open the lion's mouth" is to give him the power of speech. Here is one clue to the Great Arcanum of practical magic.

The Astral Light is also typified as a dragon, or a serpent, and the letter-name, *Teth,* means "serpent." This letter was originally pictured as a tally, suggesting counting, or measurement. Every student of Hindu philosophy knows how important counting is in many exercises for the control of *Prana* (symbolized as *Kundalini,* the coiled serpent), and students of Western magical systems will also recall many applications of a similar principle of measured, rhythmic activity. This counting is invariably an aid to concentration, and concentration is always directed to the maintenance of a selected image in the field of consciousness, without breaks or interruptions. Hence all practical methods, Eastern or Western, for controlling the Astral Light, involve the activity of the purified Imagination, typified in Strength by the woman.

She is the Empress, but the sign above her head shows that she has assimilated some of the qualities of the Magician. Readers of Hudson's works on psychic phenomena will see in her the subjective mind, purified and trained by suggestions from the objective (the Magician), mastering the Fire-principle in the human body, and so gaining control over its manifestations outside the body.

Qabalists will remember that *Hod,* the eighth Sephirah, is named "Splendor," in reference to the glory of the purified Fire-principle. They will also recall the fact that *Hod* belongs to the feminine pillar of the Tree of Life, and that its number is the sum of the numbers of *Binah,*
Understanding, and *Geburah,* Severity, the other two Sephiroth of the feminine pillar. *Hod* is the Path of Occult Intelligence, the sphere of the planet Mercury (represented in the Tarot by the Magician), and to it is attributed the element Water. In Strength the woman is Water and the lion is Fire. Thus the whole picture represents the modification of Fire and Water, and the secret of this is the Great Arcanum.

To this the name of the Path attributed to *Teth* also refers. It is "Intelligence of the Secret," or "Intelligence of all of the activities of the Spiritual Being."

Strength, then, symbolizes control of the Astral Light by Understanding; and because it is *Vau* of the formative world, it shows that such control is the equilibrating activity in all formation. In that world desire (the Lovers) takes the initiative; will (the Chariot) is the determinative principle, corresponding to the letter *Heh;* and subconscious modification of the Astral Light (Strength) maintains the balance between desire and will. Here is a great truth, expressed in simple emblems. Happy is he who can apprehend it, and happier he who has courage and patience to apply it!

CHAPTER VIII

To begin his study of the triad of trumps bearing the numbers 9, 10, and 11, let the student add the ninth and tenth cards to the tableau given in preceding chapters, thus:

$$
\begin{array}{cc}
0 & \\
1 & \\
3 & 2 \\
5 & 4 \\
6 & \\
8 & 7 \\
9 & \\
10 &
\end{array}
$$

This completes the Tree of the Sephiroth. The number 9 is Yesod, the Foundation, and 10 is
Malkuth, the Kingdom.

Yesod, spelt ISVD in Hebrew, combines the letter *Yod,* I, with word SVD, *Sod,* "a mystery." Thus the secret meaning of *Yesod* is "the mystery of *Yod."* The *Sephra Dtzenioutha* says: *"Yod* is above all (symbolizing the Father), and with him is none other associated." This doctrine is implied by the title and symbolism of the ninth trump, which also corresponds to *Yod* in the Hebrew alphabet. The Hermit lives alone, isolated; and the picture shows him "above all," on a snowy mountain-peak. His white beard suggests that he is the "Most Holy Ancient One," so often mentioned in the *Zohar;* and the gray, cowled robe recalls the name, "Concealed with all Concealment." These epithets are applied by Qabalists both to *Ain Suph* and to *Kether,* which are held to be identical in all but name. Here they refer to the correspondence between *Yesod,* the Foundation, and *Ain Suph,* the Source of all.

That correspondence will be better understood after a study of the analogies between 9, the number of *Yesod,* and 0, which symbolizes *Ain Suph.* The sign of that which precedes all manifestation is 0; and 9, the last figure in the integral series, denotes completeness, perfection, realization. The only perfect Being must be the Absolute, and the Absolute is No-thing, 0. Perfection, moreover, is beyond and above all manifestation, for manifestation is a process that ends with the realization of the Perfect. 9,

42

therefore, represents the Absolute as the Goal of all existence, while 0 typifies It as the Source of all. Consequently, in the Tarot 0 is a youth, looking upward, in the morning light; but 9 is a bearded ancient, looking down, at night. Again, the mathematical properties of 9 are similar to those of 0. Multiply any number by 9, and the product gives 9 as the least number of its reduction. Substitute 9 for 0 in a complex number, and the reduction will give the same least number. Thus 259 reduces to 7, and so does *250*. Hence, in reducing a complex number composed of several figures, 9 is regarded the same as 0, and only the other figures are added to find the least number. Finally, the extension of 9 is 45, which reduces to 9, so that 9, like 0, always produces itself by evolution.

In brief, then, the Hermit and the Fool are two aspects of one principle, which is the "foundation" of all things. The Hermit is the Ancient One, the Source of all existence, above all things, yet supporting all. He precedes everything, and is forever young, as in the symbolism of the Fool;

yet He will continue when all else has passed away, and He is the Goal of all our hopes. Thus He may be represented as a bearded ancient, the Hermit. He is shrouded in mystery; but the key to that mystery, and to all that we can apprehend concerning it, is the doctrine emphasized by Jesus, that the Absolute is the Father, or Progenitor, of all beings.

From this, by a series of deductions, we derive the idea of the Sonship of man, with its corollary of Brotherhood. From it, also, depends the hypothesis upon which all magical practice is founded, that the powers of Spirit are reproduced in man, that the difference between man and God is not one of kind, but of *degree of expression.* Hence the Hermit holds a lantern over the path, as if he were lighting the way for others making their painful journey up the mountain-side. Here is the Great Promise. In humanity are the potencies of Divinity, to be evolved by climbing the steeps of experience; and the end of the Path is union with our Source.

The tenth trump, the Wheel of Fortune, is Malkuth, the Kingdom. As the parables of Jesus plainly show, that Kingdom is not a state of life after death; nor is it, except in a very limited sense, a social order. It is *the method of Spirit in self-expression;* and because cyclicity is characteristic of that method, the Tarot symbolizes the Perfect Law as Buddha did, by a Wheel.

Around the wheel are four letters of the Roman alphabet. From left to right, beginning at the bottom, they spell the word ROTA, the Latin for "wheel." Starting from T, and reading from left to right, they form TARO. Read from right to left, beginning with 0, they spell ORAT, the present tense of the Latin verb meaning "to speak." Read in the same direction, beginning with T, the word is TORA, the phonetic equivalent of the Hebrew *Torah,* the law. And from the letter
A reading from right to left, they form ATOR, *Hathor,* the name of the Egyptian goddess corresponding to the Empress in the Tarot. Thus these four letters make a complete sentence, as follows:

ROTA TARO ORAT TORA ATOR, which may be translated thus: (The) WHEEL, TARO, SPEAKS (the) LAW (of) HATHOR.

Now, the Empress, who corresponds to Hathor, is the number 3; the sum of the numbers of the major trumps is 231; and 6, the reduction of 231, is the extension of *3.* Thus, in a sense, the whole series is summed up by the

Empress, and thus it is literally true that the Wheel of the Tarot speaks, or reveals, the Law of Hathor.

Hathor, moreover, by her connection with the Empress, corresponds to *Binah,* the third Sephirah; and because BINH, by reduction, gives the number 4, it is evident that Qabalists conceive Understanding to be represented by that number, as well as by 3. For although *4* is the number of *Chesed,* Beneficence, it is taught that *Chesed* proceeds from *Binah,* so that the potency of *Chesed* must be supposed to reside in *Binah.* I have already given some intimation of this in my
endeavors to explain how the Fatherhood of the Emperor is the consequence of the Empress'
Motherhood. The concealed significance of *Binah,* then, is connected with 4, which reminds us that the Qabalah declares the universe to be composed of four elements, manifested in four worlds, and producing four principles in the constitution of man. From 4, moreover, by extension, 10, the number of *Malkuth,* the *Kingdom,* is evolved.

To this fourfold scheme the symbolism of the Wheel of Fortune refers in various ways. It shows the four living creatures of Ezekiel and the Apocalypse – Taurus, Leo, Scorpio, and Aquarius, the second, fifth, eighth, and eleventh signs of the zodiac, the sum of whose numbers is 26, the Tetragrammaton, IHVH. This name is written on the wheel, its letters alternating with those that form the occult sentence just explained. On four arms of a double cross inscribed within the wheel are the alchemical symbols of Sulphur, Mercury, Salt, and Water. The cross itself represents the Tetragrammaton, for it has eight arms, the number given by the reduction of 26, the value of IHVH.

On the left of the wheel descends the golden serpent of the Astral Light. From its tail to its head are *ten curves.* Beginning at the tip of the tail, thirteen points are formed, including the head. Besides the various meanings of 13 mentioned in connection with the word *Binah,* is that of *unity,* because 13 is the numeration of the Hebrew word AChD, *Achad,* "one." Thus the descending serpent signifies the tenfold emanation of the One Spirit of Life.

On the right of the wheel a red Hermanubis rises. His color is that of the lion in Strength, of the Emperor's robe, and of the outer garment of the Magician.

He is one form of the Egyptian god Thoth, or Mercury, whom we have identified with the Magician. As represented here, he denotes the evolving Spirit, before it is liberated, hence he has a human body and **a** dog's head. This represents the human organism subordinated to the desire nature; but at the same time, by an analogy derived from the dog's keen scent, and his faithfulness, suggests that within the desire nature are the potencies that make for liberation.

At the top of the wheel is a Sphinx, the synthesis of the four living creatures at the corners of the picture. It remains unmoved while the wheel turns, and symbolizes liberated humanity. To show that both sexes are included in this figure, it has a man's face and a woman's breasts. For the Qabalah emphasizes the truth that though man and woman are *different,* so that each is especially qualified for certain forms of self-expression, they are at the same time equal, and necessary to each other..

Let the student now lay aside the trumps from 0 to 8, inclusive, and place 11 with 9 and 10, so that it bears to 10 the same relation that 2 does to 1 on the Tree of the Sephiroth. I need not elaborate, upon the similarities between Justice and the High Priestess, for they will be apparent to the most casual observer. But because Evolution is the reverse of Involution, the details of the eleventh card offer certain contrasts to those of the second. Thus the hair of Justice is yellow, while that of the High Priestess is black; and the High Priestess' robe is blue, but Justice is clad in red, like the Emperor.

Her sword suggests the same ideas as the letter *Zain,* which corresponds to the Lovers. It implies division, separation, classification, and the like; and all these are connected with the occult meaning of the duad, of which Justice is a symbol, because her number, 11, reduces to 2. She is the aspect of *Chokmah,* Wisdom, that analyzes, separates things into their component parts, weighs and measures, and so discovers the workings of nature. Her purpose is the adjustment of man to his environment, and the modification and improvement of all the conditions of that environment, through the intelligent direction of natural forces according to their laws. Justice, therefore, is a deduction from the Wheel of Fortune. She symbolizes the practical application of the law of action and reaction implied in the doctrine of cycles. In a sense she typifies the Law of Karma, since the primitive meaning of Karma is "Action"; and in this connection it should be observed that the *Sepher Yetzirah* attributes Work, or Action, to *Lamed,* her correspondence in

the Hebrew alphabet. *Lamed* is the "ox-goad," symbolizing the means whereby the "Ox" *(Aleph,* the Fool), is guided and directed. In other words, the action of evolving humanity (and action, be it remembered, includes thought and speech), gives tendency, or definite purpose to the manifestation of the limitless possibilities of the Absolute.

This is a cardinal doctrine of the Ancient Wisdom, and all sacred writings elaborate it. As the Psalmist says, man is "but a little lower than God," and all things are under his feet; because he is a center of expression for Absolute Wisdom and Limitless Power, able to discover the laws of the universe in which he lives, and able, also, to adapt those laws by his thought, his words, and his works, so as to produce better conditions than those provided by nature unmodified by the introduction of the human personal factor.

CHAPTER IX

Concerning the twelfth Key of the Tarot, which is the first of the triad to be studied in this chapter, I have recently received, from an eminent occultist whose knowledge of the Qabalah and the Tarot is very profound, the following statement:

"The correct geometrical figure concealed by the Hanged Man is the Cross, surmounting a Water Triangle. It signifies the multiplication of the tetrad by the triad. This is the number 12. The 'door,' *Daleth,* is the vehicle of the tetrad, for it **is** the Great Womb also; and the head of the Hanged Man reflected therein, is the LVX, in manifestation as the Logos. He is Osiris, Sacrifice, and *Yod-Heh-Shins-Vav-Heh, Yehoshua.*"

Advanced occultists will require no further explanation of the twelfth trump, but as the present work is designed primarily for beginners, I shall elaborate somewhat upon the foregoing exposition. It is obvious, of course, that the legs of the Hanged Man form a cross, and that lines drawn from his elbows to the point formed by his hair will form the sides of a reversed triangle having his arms for its base. The cross is the number 4, and it refers to the Emperor. By his connection with the letter *Heh* in the Hebrew alphabet, the Emperor corresponds to the sign Aries, the head of the Fire triplicity in the Zodiac. Hence the legs of the Hanged Man are red, the color of Fire. In contrast to them, the upper part of his body is clad in blue, to represent Water which, as has been said, is also represented by the reversed triangle. The latter also denotes the number 3, or the Empress, who is *Binah,* the "root of Water." Thus the geometrical basis of the picture is a symbol of the multiplication of the fiery power of the Emperor, who is an aspect of Purusha, by the generative power of the Universal Feminine Principle. The arithmetical symbol of this process is the number 12, or *4* multiplied by *3*; and since 12 is the number of the signs of the Zodiac, it denotes a complete cycle or' manifestation. Hence we may say that the Hanged Man symbolizes the whole Law of Manifestation.

The number 12 is also a symbol of the union of 1 and 2, or the Magician and the High Priestess. The cross formed by the legs of the Hanged Man thus refers to the four elements which the Magician arranges and classifies,. and it is red, to correspond to the Magician's robe, Similarly the upper garment of the Hanged Man is like that of the High Priestess, and on some versions of the twelfth trump this garment is decorated with crescents representing the waxing and waning moon.

Because 12 reduces to 3, the Hanged Man corresponds to the Empress. This correspondence has been partly explained in the preceding paragraphs, but it is strengthened by the fact that the twelfth trump symbolizes the Hebrew letter *Mem,* which is the symbol of Water – the second of the three "Mother" letters in the alphabet, to which are assigned the elements Air, Water and Fire – and the Empress, as *Binah,* is the "root of water."

The cross from which he is suspended suggests the letter *Tau,* to which is assigned the final trump of the Tarot series. The title of this last card is "The World," and its symbolism in many respects is the exact reverse of that of the Hanged Man, even as its number, 21, reverses the figures that form 12. This final Key symbolizes the totality of manifestation, and the Perfect Law at work therein. Hence the Hanged Man may be regarded as "He who is dependent upon the *Tau* of the Perfect Law." What this means will become a little clearer when it is known that the geometrical basis of the Hanged Man is also the ancient occult symbol of Personality. Thus it will be seen that the central doctrine of the twelfth Key is this: "Personal existence is wholly dependent upon the totality of manifestation."

To exemplify this truth, and to demonstrate it, the Logos becomes incarnate – not once only, but in various ages of the world's history. Hence the Hanged Man is both Osiris and Yehoshua (Jesus). He is the Agnus Dei, who is "one with the Father." That Father, in the Tarot, is the Emperor, the Ram, Aries, who is the Fire-god, Agni, of the Hindus. From Him the Logos or Son, proceeds, and yet that Son, who is the "fulfilling of the Law," declares, according to the New Testament, "Of myself I can do nothing."

Hence we see the Hanged Man bound, as a type of sacrifice, and as a symbol of the doctrine that personality is absolutely dependent upon the totality of manifestation. This doctrine, at first glance, appears to support the philosophy of determinism; but really it does nothing of the kind. What it does declare is that personality is not the source of Will, but the vehicle of the Divine Initiative. The corollary of this doctrine is that the Perfect Law Affords adequate support for personal existence. Hence we may safely surrender the whole of our life, from hour to hour, and from day to day, to the guidance of the Supreme Spirit, which is the true I AM, the "Ego seated in the hearts of men."

The thirteenth trump is associated with the letter *Nun,* which means "a fish."

49

This symbol, closely identified with the Christian secret doctrine, denotes life in water. In the Tarot sequence this is life in *Mem,* or life dependent upon other modes of existence. It is ever-changing and temporal. In contrast to eternal Life, therefore, it is Death. The Qabalistic Path assigned to *Nun* is Imaginative Intelligence, or knowledge that takes form in mental images. The letter *Nun* is also said to be derived from a hieroglyphic representing a fruit of any kind. Now, every mental image is a fruit, or synthesis, of previous thinking, and each image is the seed of others. All images are temporary and subject to development and modification. By imagination old truths take newer forms, and the latent possibilities of familiar things are discovered. Imagination, therefore, is the great transforming power that alters everything in our world. It is the agency whereby the Supreme Spirit reveals to us the infinite possibilities that surround us, and thus is it the vehicle of the Divine Beneficence. The latter is *Chesed,* the Sephirah corresponding to the number 4, and the reduction of 13 is 4. Now, the production of new forms of manifestation through the operation of the Imaginative Intelligence involves the passing away of older forms, in order to give place to the new. Every new invention, for example, throws countless old devices upon the scrap-heap. Hence the Tarot pictures the Imaginative Intelligence either as a reaping skeleton, or as a skeleton rider upon a white horse. The latter is Mr. Waite's version. The horse represents the Eternal Progress of the Universal Radiant Energy in Evolution. Before its rider a king has fallen, to symbolize the passing away of the ancient delusion that authority is vested by divine right in a hereditary royalty. A priest, a woman, and a child are about to fall. They are the old false notions about religion, the status of women, and the rights of children. All these things shall pass away before the advance of new ideals, developed in the race consciousness by the transforming power of Imagination. In the background a sun is rising between two pillars. Readers who have a pack of Tarot cards should compare this with the eighteenth trump. It is the promise of a New Day, dawning beyond the watch-towers of the Known.

The fourteenth Key combines the ideas of the twelfth and the thirteenth, for it is the *Vau* that unites the *Yod* of the Hanged Man to the *Heh* of Death. Its number, 14, combines the ideas represented by the Magician (1) and the Emperor (4); and these are resumed in the number *5,* which is the reduction of 14. Hence Temperance may be taken to represent ideas analogous to those of the Hierophant.

The angel, in Mr. Waite's version, seems to be male; but it is more often represented in older Tarots as a female figure, and is sometimes taken to represent the goddess Diana. In reality it is androgyne, for it is the Supreme Spirit, the Universal Father-Mother. Hence, in Mr. Waite's design, careful scrutiny will show the Tetragrammaton, *Yod-Heh-Vau-Heh*, embroidered in Hebrew letters on the collar of the angel's robe.

Below the Tetragrammaton is a Fire Triangle enclosed in a square. This refers to the manifestation of the Fire of Spirit through the Square of Matter. It is also an intimation of the working of the power represented in the Tarot by the Chariot, or the number Seven, through the agency of the duad., For the number 14 is 7 multiplied by 2. In Temperance the duad is typified by the two cups, which are analogous to the pillars of the High Priestess, to the Man and Woman in the Lovers, and to the two ministers kneeling before the Hierophant. The cups are Purusha (right-hand) and Prakriti (left-hand) manifested in human consciousness as what modern psychologists term the objective and the subjective minds.

The triple stream of water which the angel pours from one cup to the other is the stream of personal consciousness, which passes from the inner life of the subjective mind into the outer life of the objective. In that outer life the ideas received from subjective mentation are put to the test of action. Hence the Path connected with Temperance through the letter *Samekh* is called "Tentative Intelligence," or the "Intelligence of Probation," to indicate the principal function of the objective mind, which is the testing of ideas, received from within, by putting them to work
in the outer plane. The student should note that the current flows from the inner consciousness, or left-hand cup, in response to an impulse received from the angel, or Supreme Spirit; and he should also observe that the power of the objective mind to receive, formulate, and test these ideas coming from the subjective mind is not its own, but something dependent upon the perfect Wisdom of the Higher Self.

The water that is poured from cup to cup has been dipped up from the pool of Universal Life, and the long path leading from the pool to the mountain-peak in the distance is the same as that which brought the Fool to the peak whereon he stands before descending into the Abyss of Manifestation. The end thereof, above which shines a crown, a symbol of *Kether,* the Primal Will, is the height attained by the Hermit. It is union with the Supreme Spirit, the Goal of occult study and practice. We shall meet with this symbol of the Path again in the eighteenth Key. Need I say that it refers to the doctrine of reincarnation, and that the little stream of Water from the pool, which the angel pours from cup to cup, is an emblem of a single life?

CHAPTER X

The significance of the fifteenth Tarot Key has little, if anything to do with that creature of the gloomy imaginations of mediaeval theology – the malignant personal adversary of mankind, who bought human souls and presided at the *Sabbat*. In a certain sense, to be sure, it is the tempter and deceiver of man, and although it is not the devil of theologians, it does correspond to that which is called the "Devil" in the Bible. Primarily, however, this trump denotes a particular aspect of the Great Magical Agent, concerning which Eliphas Levi wrote:
"It is the first physical manifestation of the Divine Breath. God creates it eternally, and man, in
the image of the Deity, modifies and apparently multiplies it in the reproduction of his species."

This doctrine of Western occultism is identical with the Yoga teaching that the Divine Breath (Prana) is especially active in the reproductive centers of the human organism. The Yogis assert that this energy in the sex-centers may be transmuted into the "illuminating or bright" force which they call *Ojas,* the very highest form of Prana. Ojas, they say, working through certain high centers of the nervous system, brings about the liberation of the mind from the illusions of sense-life.

In his correspondence to the generative aspect of the Great Magical Agent, the Devil is also related to the Greek god, Priapus, the son of Dionysos and Aphrodite. Dionysos was known in the Eleusinian mysteries as Iacchos. He is represented in the Tarot by the Fool and the Hermit. Aphrodite, as we know, is the Empress. Hence we may say that the Devil, as Priapus, is the projection of the ideas represented by the Fool, the Empress, and the Hermit. *All these trumps correspond to the letter Yod in the Tetragrammaton,* and, with the exception of the Fool, they all bear numbers which are multiples of 3. Furthermore, the number of the Devil is 15, which is the extension of 5, the number of the Hierophant; and the reduction of 15 is 6, the number of the Lovers. The student should carefully compare the symbolism of the Devil with all of these trumps.

By its correspondence to the letter *Ayin,* this card is also related to Capricorn, and the Devil's horns refer to that correspondence. Capricorn is the nocturnal house of Saturn. In alchemy "Saturn" is lead, and the

nocturnal house of Saturn corresponds to the *dark state of lead,* i. e., to the state of the metal *before transmutation.* The untransmuted lead is the Vital Light in the
nerve-centers controlling reproduction. Hence, in one attribution of the metals to the Sephiroth, we find Lead ascribed to *Yesod,* the Foundation, which is associated in the Qabalah with the reproductive power of Microprosopus.

These hints should be sufficient to set the student upon the track of the true interpretation of the fifteenth Key; but perhaps the meaning will be even clearer if I add another quotation from the eminent Qabalist whose explanation of the Hanged Man was given in Chapter IX. He says:

"The Devil is a figure of the Creative Fire encased in Matter, and he is also the god of 'them that walk in darkness.' For they see the Source of All as a creative power ungoverned by Law; but God follows the Law of His own being, which is Love. Love misunderstood, materialized, and perverted, is the veritable Devil. Therefore are the human figures in chains, and the Pentagram inverted."

By its connection with the letter *Peh,* the sixteenth major trump corresponds to the planet Mars, which rules Aries by day and Scorpio by night. Aries is the Emperor, and Scorpio is Death. These two cards are also connected with the Tower, because they correspond to the first *Heh* in the Tetragrammaton. In the same way, too, the Tower corresponds to the Magician, whose
number is the final reduction of the extension of 16 (136=10=1); to the Chariot, whose number is the reduction of 16; and to the Wheel of Fortune, whose number is the first reduction of the extension of 16.

In the symbolism of this trump, Mars is the lightning flash which denotes the masculine aspect of Spirit or Purusha. Hence Krishna says, "Among weapons I am the thunder-bolt." Among the ancients lightning was an emblem of fecundation and nutrition, as well as of destruction; and Plutarch says, "The agriculturalists call the lightning the fertilizer of the waters, and so regard it." *(Symposiacs.* IV. 2.) Here we are reminded of the Greek myth that Ares (Mars) was the lover and consort of Aphrodite.

The lightning flash is the power drawn from above by the Magician; the sceptre of the Emperor; the sword of the Charioteer (and, in one sense, the

Charioteer himself); the force that turns the Wheel of Fortune; the scythe of Death. It forever breaks down existing forms in order to make room for new ones. The Tower is the garden of the Magician; the throne of the Emperor; the Chariot; the Turning Wheel; the figures that fall before Death. It is the universal feminine principle, Prakriti. Sometimes it is called "The House of God;" that is. "The abode of Spirit," or Prakriti conceived as the vehicle of Purusha.

When we see that Prakriti is a vehicle, and not a separate entity, we perceive that, from moment to moment, throughout all time, it is always being transformed. Hence the sixteenth trump represents a process that continues during the entire course of manifestation. In its application to human life, this picture shows the result of the realization of the true nature of Self, concerning which the Hindu teachers of one school say, "True knowledge makes Prakriti disappear, first as containing Purusha, and then as separate from Purusha."[8]

The falling figures correspond to the chained prisoners of the fifteenth card. They fall headfirst, because the sudden influx of spiritual consciousness suggested by the lightning flash completely upsets all our old notions of the relations between Purusha and Prakriti, and these two are Purusha and Prakriti as the objective and subjective modes of human consciousness.

In one sense this picture denotes the second stage of spiritual unfoldment, in which, by a series of sudden, fitful inspirations, the student perceives the illusive nature of his sense of personal separateness, and suffers thereby the destruction of his whole previous philosophy. And in yet another, although closely related aspect, the sixteenth Key depicts the overthrow of the folly of men by the wisdom of God; which is allegorically represented in the Old Testament story of the Tower of Babel and the confusion of tongues.

The seventeenth Key, through its correspondence to *Tzaddi,* represents the sign Aquarius, which is the diurnal throne of Saturn. Thus the Star is the antithesis of the Devil, and represents the transmuted "lead," or the *bright state* of the reproductive force; and as the transmuted lead is gold, corresponding astrologically to the Sun, so is the light of the great star, which shines above the kneeling woman, the light of a distant sun.

By its correspondence to *Vau* in the Tetragrammaton, the Star is related to the

8 Mohini Chatterji, *The Lord's Lay,* p. 217.

54

High Priestess, the Hierophant, Strength, Justice, and Temperance. It corresponds particularly to Strength, because the reduction of 17 is **8**.

The great star is Sirius, the star of Isis-Sothis, and the seven smaller stars are the seven planets of ancient astronomy, which are also the seven metals of the alchemists, and the seven great centers of Prana in the human body. The kneeling figure is a synthesis of Isis, Nephthys, and Hathor. There is an aspect, too, in which she represents Nuit, the Egyptian goddess of heaven. In this aspect she corresponds to Aquarius, the water-bearer, for Nuit is the atmosphere, exercising its double function of holding Water in suspension, and pouring it out on land and sea.

One leg rests upon the earth, the other upon the water; and in this particular she repeats the symbolism of the angel of Temperance. Her two vases resemble the cups he holds, and they are also analogous to the pillars of the High Priestess, of the Hierophant, and of Justice. She, herself, is the woman of Strength, the Universal Feminine Principle, unveiled, because she represents a phase of consciousness in which the real nature of the "mysterious power" is perceived, though dimly, as by starlight.

The streams of water are the currents of the Astral Fluid. The student should observe that all the water comes from the pool. Some of it returns directly, from the right-hand vase, to symbolize the positive, direct action of the Astral Fluid when the highest manifestation of Prakriti, *Buddhi*, presents truth to us through Intuition. The stream from the left-hand vase is divided into five
parts after it reaches the earth, and symbolizes the indirect perception of truth through the senses.

The figure of the woman also suggests by its attitude a swastika, or fylfot cross. This cross is particularly related to the number 17, because a fylfot cross based upon a magic square of
twenty-five cells, contains seventeen cells. This cross is a most ancient symbol, and is known to occultists as a synthesis of the whole creation.

A feature of the seventeenth trump, as it appears in Mr. Waite's Tarot, which would be quite likely to escape the eyes of an uninitiated observer, is the apparently haphazard arrangement of ten small plants scattered here and there on the ground near the edge of the pool. These are the ten Sephiroth, and they correspond to the design embroidered upon the veil behind the High Priestess.

Finally, through its correspondence to *Tzaddi,* as the reader will see by referring to the Table in Chapter III, the Star is an emblem of meditation. It is the *Dhyana* of the Yoga philosophers, a continuous dwelling upon one idea, a diving into the depths of the mind for ideas associated with a central thought, which Patanjali calls, "an unbroken flow of knowledge in a particular object." This is the third stage in the unfoldment of spiritual consciousness.

CHAPTER XI

The eighteenth major trump, the Moon, symbolizes the various Qabalistic attributions of *Qoph,*
tabulated in Chapter 3. Since *Qoph,* the number 100, corresponds by reduction to *10 = Yod* and *1 = Aleph,* the Moon is analogous to the Hermit and the Fool. All three cards represent the Path of Manifestation. The Fool is the Beginning of the Way; the Hermit is the Goal of the Journey; and the Moon is the Path of Unfoldment, beginning in the Water of the Abyss, and ascending gradually to heights far beyond the Watch-towers of the Known.

In the eighteenth Key, Spirit is symbolized by the crayfish; partly because, after descending into manifestation, Spirit begins its evolution in various forms of water life; and partly because the crayfish is a symbol analogous to the Egyptian scarabaeus, Khephra, god of the rising sun, creator of all, "father of the gods."

The Path rises from a pool, similar to those of Temperance and the Star; and as it passes over rolling country, it is a succession of ascents and descents, and not a straight up-grade. This refers to a psychological law, at work in all evolution, which is of particular importance to occultists. A modern work on business psychology explains this law in language so like the symbolism of the eighteenth Key that one might almost think the author a Tarot student. He says, describing what happens when one takes up a new line of work, that great progress is usually made at first, because the first steps "are made largely by merely using old habits and previously acquired skill or knowledge, and reorganizing and adapting them to new uses." After a time, just when the first enthusiasm begins to wane, further advance requires the formation of new habits. "For a time
one seems to make no advance in skill, He may even become less successful in the performance. He has reached what is known as a plateau in habit formation.

"When a plateau of arrested progress has been reached, the faint-hearted become discouraged and quit. However, the knowledge that their experience is a normal one should give them resolution to keep on. When a plateau has been reached, further progress depends mainly on the ability to hold one's self to the task by sheer force of will, until the new knowledge is assimilated, the new habits are formed, and the new skill is developed." [9]

This law of habit formation is one of the results of the universal Law of Rhythm which pervades all phases of evolution.

All things have their ebb and flow, their elevation and depression, their pendulum-like swing between opposite poles. Hence the dominant symbol of this Key is the Moon, which represents the Law of Rhythm by its phases, and by its influence upon the tides. It is also directly related to the High Priestess, who is Prakriti, the Universal Subjective Mind.

The Path of Attainment, whether racial or personal, is a series of developments brought about through the agency of the subjective mind, which is the seat of habit, controls all the functions of the body, and effects all structural modifications. It follows, though the doctrine may seem materialistic until one is familiar with all that it includes, *that the point of evolution reached by any person is determined by the structure of his body,* and, similarly, that the point of racial evolution is determined by the *average* structure of the bodies of the persons composing the race.

On one side of the Path is a wolf, on the other a dog. In Egyptian mythology these are the jackals of Anubis; but they have another meaning, of great practical interest to all who seek to follow the Ancient Way. The dog and the wolf are of the same genus, but the wolf is wild, while the dog is
a domesticated animal. The wolf represents natural conditions; the dog denotes the same conditions, transformed by the intelligent application of the human will. Broadly speaking, therefore, the wolf is a symbol for Nature, and the dog a symbol for Art. The Path lies between, to show that true progress depends upon the maintenance of a proper equilibrium between the crudities of uncontrolled Nature on the one hand, and the over-refinements of artificiality on the other.

In the middle distance are the Watch-towers of the East and the West. They are the Pillars of the High Priestess, and the Pillars of Mercy and Severity on the Qabalistic Tree of Life. The Path between corresponds to the Pillar of Mildness. Hence the Path itself represents the Qabalistic synthesis of Divine Wisdom, the Divine Name, *Yod-Heh-Vau-Heh,* because the numbers of the

---

9 Psychology for Business Efficiency. George R. Eastman. p. 30.

Sephiroth on the Pillar of Mildness total 26, the number of the Tetragrammaton.

Beyond the Pillars lies the great region of the Unknown, through which the Path leads to the great height whereon the Hermit stands. It is the eminence which, in Temperance, is surmounted by a crown, the symbol of *Kether.* The region beyond the Pillars is wild and uncultivated, in contrast to the green field of the Known in the foreground. This implies that we must first traverse the known, and establish our equilibrium between Nature and Art therein, before attempting to scale the more difficult heights beyond.

Finally, the eighteenth Key also corresponds to the fourth stage in the unfoldment of spiritual consciousness. The first stage was the darkness and bondage of the Devil; the second, the fitful, though brilliant, lightning-flashes of intuition, that destroy the sense of separateness; the third, the dim starlight of the calm meditation that follows the storm of the second stage. The fourth stage is that of conscious advance along the Path; but although the light is brighter than the starlight, it is reflected, and it waxes and wanes.

In contrast to it, the nineteenth Key shows the direct, steady radiance of the Sun. Mr. Waite's version of this trump is a variant given by Eliphas Levi, who interprets it as "the will of the adept," and connects it with the following passage in the Chaldean Oracles of Zoroaster:
"Let us go further, and affirm the existence of a Fire which abounds in images and reflections. Term it, if you will, a superabundant light which radiates, which speaks, which goes back into itself. It is the flaming courser of light, or rather it is the stalwart child who overcomes and breaks in that heavenly steed. Picture him as vested in flame and emblazoned with gold, or think of him naked as love, and bearing the arrows of' Eros."[10]

Because 19=10=1, the Sun corresponds to the Magician, or *Kether;* and since *Kether* is the goal of the Path in the Moon, the child of the nineteenth Key represents the realization of personal identity with the Primal Will which is the end of conscious development. It is in this sense that the child is "the will of the adept." His horse, a domesticated animal, symbolizes the solar force, after it has been specialized and adapted to the realization of purposes determined by the selective power of the adept's will.

---

10 History of Magic. Translated by A. E. Waite. p. 56.

Because he is *Kether,* and *Kether* is identical with *Ain Suph* (the Fool) in all but name, the child has the same fair hair as the Fool; and from a wreath on his head rises the Fool's red feather. The wreath is of flowers, to represent the perfection of the Great Work, to accomplish which the Fool descends; even as the metal Gold, symbolized by the Sun, is the alchemical emblem of the perfection of that same work. Because the operation is accomplished through a cycle of time, the flowers of the wreath are twelve in number, to correspond to the jewels of the Fool's girdle. Here also is an allusion to the symbolism of the Wheel of Fortune, which is also analogous to the Sun. In contrast to the Fool, the child is naked; for, if "the Spirit clothes itself to come down," as Qabalists declare, it must unclothe itself to go up.

The child is the Ego, set free from the limitations of matter and circumstance, which are symbolized by the wall behind him. He is master of the solar light (the horse), and the terrestrial fire (the red banner). He is the personification of the power of the Sun which shines above him, hence the sunflowers on the wall turn toward the child. The rays of the Sun, alternately waved and salient, symbolize the alternation of the two natures, Purusha and Prakriti, male and female, objective and subjective.

This whole Key symbolizes the fifth stage of spiritual development, in which the adept, though freed from the limitations of circumstance, and conscious of his essential identity with the Supreme Spirit, nevertheless feels himself to be a separate, or at least, distinct, entity. This is not full liberation; but it is a very much higher state than any of those before it.

Mr. Waite's version of the twentieth Key seems less happy than any of his other departures from the ancient symbolism. The three figures in the background are particularly confusing, and I shall ignore them in my interpretation.

Since it corresponds to *Shin,* the letter of Fire, this Key symbolizes the occult doctrine about that element. The Supernal Creative Fire manifests itself in the Divine Breath, *Ruach Elohim,* and Qabalists call attention to the fact that the total of the letter values in *Ruach Elohim* (RVCh ALHIM) is 300, the number of *Shin.*

That Divine Breath is the angel of the twentieth Key. He is the Universal Creative Fire, concentrated in solar force. His hair is red and yellow, to suggest the mingling of Fire (red) and Air (yellow). His blue robe, like that of the High Priestess, refers to *Chokmah,* the second Sephirah, which is "the root of Fire." His trumpet denotes the manifestation of the Cosmic Fire through Sound. Close scrutiny will show seven lines descending from the trumpet. These are the seven modifications of the Great Breath; the seven *Tattvas* of esoteric Hinduism; the seven Spirits of God; the seven "double" letters of the Hebrew alphabet. The cross on the banner refers to the letters of the Tetragrammaton, to the four elements, the four Qabalistic worlds, and the four rivers of Eden. It also relates to the Path in the eighteenth Key, because that Path is the Pillar of Mildness, corresponding to the Tetragrammaton.

The influence poured from the trumpet is received by the outstretched arms of the woman. She should be shown rising from water, for she symbolizes the fluidic and passive Fire, AVB, Ob. AVB = 1, 6, 2 = 9 = Teth = Strength. This woman rising from the water is she who tames the lion in the eighth Key. She corresponds also to the waved rays of the Sun in the nineteenth Key.

Opposite her a man rises from the earth. He is the active and terrestrial Fire, AVD, Od. AVD = 1, 6, 4 = 11 = 2 = Beth = the Magician. The man is the dominant figure of the first Key, and he corresponds to the salient rays of the Sun.

His hands are folded, because in the stage of evolution here depicted, the objective consciousness which he symbolizes remains comparatively inactive, for it is fixed in its contemplation of the Supreme Spirit. While the objective consciousness is thus held in restraint, so to speak, the subjective consciousness receives the seven-fold influx of power direct from its Supernal Source.

The child is the regenerated personality, rising from the tomb of material existence. His back is toward us, because he represents return to the Source of All. For this Key is the sixth stage of the Path, in which personal consciousness is on the verge of blending with the Universal. At this stage the adept realizes that his personal existence is nothing but the manifestation of the relation between the two natures of the Supreme Spirit (the woman and the man); that it has no separate existence in reality. The light that shines here is beyond that of the Sun or Moon. It neither waxes and wanes, nor does it rise and set. It is the unfailing light of the Fire of Divine Wisdom, which consumes all falsehood, and purges the whole life of the aspirant.

CHAPTER XII

The last of the twenty-two major trumps, the World, shows a female figure, in the midst of an elliptical wreath. Her hair is yellow, like that of the Empress, to whom she also corresponds, through the number 21, which reduces to 3. She is nude, save for a light scarf. Her legs are crossed, like those of the Hanged Man; and her arms form the sides of a triangle having her head for its apex, and an imaginary line connecting her hands for its base. She therefore represents a triangle surmounting a cross, and repeats the symbolism of the seventh trump, explained in Chapter VII. This is the reverse of the symbolism of the Hanged Man, even as the number 21 is the reverse of 12. In each hand she holds a light wand, to indicate the equilibrium of the positive and negative currents of the Great Magical Agent. At the four corners of the card, outside the wreath, are the four living creatures of Ezekiel and the Apocalypse.

In older versions of the World, the scarf which is the central figure's only covering suggests the shape of the letter *Kaph,* and so indicates a connection between the twenty-first Key and the tenth. Another clue pointing in the same direction is the fact that the World, through the letter *Tau,* corresponds to the thirty-second Path of the *Sepher Yetzirah,* which begins in Yesod, the ninth Sephirah, or the Hermit, and ends in Malkuth, the tenth, which corresponds by its number to the Wheel of Fortune. To emphasize this connection between the World and the Wheel of Fortune. Mr. Waite has put the four living creatures at the corners of the tenth Key also; but this is a departure from the original symbolism. The wheel in the tenth trump is analogous to the ellipse of the twenty-first; for when the ellipse is correctly drawn, it gives a key to the quadrature of the circle, as derived by ancient geometricians from the 3-4-5 right-angled triangle.

This quadrature is not mathematically exact, but it has an important symbolical meaning. In occult parlance "to square the circle" is to establish a perfect equilibrium between Spirit, the circle, and Matter, the square. That same equilibrium is indicated in several ways in the twenty- first Key; by the perfect balance of the central figure, although her feet rest on nothing more solid than air (an intimation, too, that her support is Spirit, *Ruach,* Air); by the two wands; and by the triangle surmounting the cross, which is the geometrical basis of the central figure. It is also very subtly suggested by the wreath itself, for the ellipse, unlike a circle, has two distinct *sides,* and these are analogous to the pillars of the High Priestess, joined at top and bottom, to show the union of Mercy and Severity. Again, the wreath is held together at top and bottom by the lemniscate symbol which hovers above the heads of the Magician and the woman in Strength, and this, too, is an emblem of magical equilibrium. That equilibrium is also implied by the number 21, which combines 2, the duad, or Matter, with 1, the monad, or Spirit. The same idea is suggested by the ancient form of the letter *Tau,* to which the World corresponds. This was a cross, in which the vertical line denoted Spirit, and the horizontal line, Matter. Spirit is the *subject* of manifestation, Purusha; Matter is the *object,* Prakriti. The quadrature of the circle, then, in the language of occult psychology, is the merging of the subjective and objective modes of consciousness into that higher consciousness, transcending subject and object, which is the Goal of all mystical aspiration. The term "Cosmic Consciousness," sometimes applied to this thought-transcending realization, corresponds exactly to the title of the twenty-first Key.

In that Key, according to some interpreters of the Tarot, the central figure is androgyne; and the scarf conceals this fact. Eliphas Levi hints at the same thing when he identifies this figure with Truth; for he also says that the androgyne Hindu symbol, *Ardha-Nari,* represents Truth, and is equivalent to the Adonai of Ezekiel's vision. Readers of *The Perfect Way* will recall Anna Kingsford's description of this Vision of Adonai, which she calls "the most stupendous fact of mystical experience, and the crowning experience of seers in all ages from the remotest antiquity to the present day." Her words are particularly significant when we recall that the twenty-first trump is sometimes . entitled "The Crown of the Magi." Perhaps I can offer no better commentary upon this Key than Dr. Kingsford's account of that sublime vision.

"He (the seer) finds himself amid a company innumerable of beings manifestly divine; for they are the angels and archangels, principalities and powers, and all the hierarchy of the 'Heavens.' Pressing on, through these towards the centre, he next finds himself in presence of a light so intolerable in its lustre as well-nigh to beat him back from further quest,.....

"Enshrined in this light is a Form radiant and glorious beyond all power of expression. For it is 'made of the Substance of Light'; and the form is that of the 'Only Begotten,' the Logos, the Idea, the Manifestor of God, the Personal Reason of all existence, the Lord God of Hosts, the Lord Adonai. From the right hand upraised in attitude indicative of will and command, proceeds, as a stream of living force, the Holy Life and Substance whereby and whereof Creation consists.

With the left hand, depressed and open as in attitude of recall, the stream is indrawn, and Creation is sustained and redeemed. Thus projecting and recalling, expanding and contracting, Adonai fulfils the functions expressed in the mystical formula *Solve et Coagula.* And as in this, so also in constitution and form, Adonai is dual, comprising the two modes of humanity, and appearing to the beholder alternately masculine and feminine according as the function exercised is of the man or the woman, and is centrifugal or centripetal." [11]

The number 21 is the extension of 6, the number of the Lovers. The sixth trump corresponds to *Zain,* and the value of *Zain* is 7. Now, the extension of 7 is 28, and that of 28 is 406, the number given by the letter-name *Tau* (ThV). In the ancient version of the seventh trump, reproduced in Papus' *Tarot of the Bohemians,* the letters V and T are enclosed in the shield on the face of the Chariot; and they are, of course, to be read from right to left, so as to spell *Tau.* In Oswald Wirth's Tarot these letters are replaced by one form of the Hindu *lingam,* and Mr. Waite uses a variant of the same symbolism. I prefer the older form, because it so clearly indicates the correspondence between the World and the Chariot, in addition to the identity of the geometrical basis of the seventh and twenty-first Keys, which is a triangle surmounting a cross. The number 21 also connects the World with the Chariot, as well as with the Lovers, for 21 is 7 times 3, and so indicates the manifestation of the power of the Empress through that of the Chariot. The Empress is *Binah,* and the Chariot is *Netzach.* Hence, by its number, 7 times 3, the World symbolizes the final Victory of Understanding, or the triumph of the power of *Binah* over all the illusions of material life.

Tau corresponds also to Saturn, who is described in mythology as devouring his children. Even so does the highest of all mystical experiences swallow up the lower forms of knowing in the superconsciousness that Hindus term "Existence – Knowledge – Bliss – Absolute. "In like manner, too, does that element which Hindus represent as an ellipse – the Akasha Tattva – swallow up the other four elements, and unite all sensation in the inner Hearing. For the Vision of Adonai is accompanied by a Voice, and that Voice is the utterance of the Soundless Sound, the Logos of Infinite Space. Here I approach that of which it is not lawful to speak; not because any rule imposes silence, but rather because the laws of language make unintelligible any attempt to formulate, in words coined to describe the normal experience of mankind, something which so far transcends our

---

11 The Perfect Way, Lecture IX, 49, 50, 51.